A CIVILIAN AFFAIR

A BRIEF HISTORY OF THE
CIVILIAN AIRCRAFT COMPANY OF HEDON

G-ABNT

EDUARD F. WINKLER

FLIGHT RECORDER PUBLICATIONS

A passion for accuracy

First published in Great Britain in 2003 by
Flight Recorder Publications Ltd
Ashtree House, Station Road, Ottringham,
East Yorkshire, HU12 0BJ
Tel: 01964 624223 Fax: 01964 624666
E-mail: beketley@dircon.co.uk
Website: www.flight-recorder.com
© 2003 Flight Recorder Publications Ltd

ISBN 0 9545605 0 7

Edited by Barry Ketley
Design by Flight Recorder Publications Ltd
Printed in England

Caption to title page: *A recent view of the sole surviving Civilian Coupe Mk II, G-ABNT. This is the third of only five aircraft to be completed and was granted its first C of A on 10 September 1931. It was rebuilt to award-winning Concours standard by Tony Habgood between 1978 and 1980.*

2 Above: Seen in July 1929, this is the team responsible for the design and construction of the very first Civilian Coupé in front of the aircraft in the yard of the brewery engineers, Samuel Briggs and Company, of Moor Street, Burton on Trent. The man with his hands in his pockets is A.P. Hunt, while next to him with his hand on the propeller hub is the design leader, and founder of the company, Harold Boultbee. Typically, he looks rather grim faced. Comparison with the men shows how small the Coupé was. The other men are believed to be employees of Briggs who worked on the aircraft. Could it be that the aircraft's registration, G-AAIL, was intended to be pronounced to rhyme with 'ale'?

Aviation can be said to have really begun in the Hull area when the noted British aviator, Gustav Hamel, made a series of demonstration flights over the surrounding area from the racecourse at Hedon on Saturday 13 July 1912. His aircraft, a Blériot monoplane, was similar to that in which the first aerial crossing of the English Channel had been made (by Louis Blériot on 25 July 1909). These flights, and the numerous attempts by W.H. Ewen to fly to Hull, were the subjects of many breathless reports in the *Hull Daily Mail*.

Although these early aerial escapades were some of the first in the Hull area, Yorkshire has a long history of pioneering aviation achievements, notably the experiments by Sir George Cayley of Brompton by Sawdon, near Scarborough, who is unquestionably the father of heavier-than-air flight. These experiments began as early as 1796 when he designed a flying model helicopter. In 1849 he designed a glider which carried a ten-year old boy aloft. This was followed by a larger glider which was flown by Cayley's coachman(!) in 1853. The results of Cayley's experimental analysis in defining the forces which act upon an aircraft, namely lift, gravity, thrust and drag, were the vital conclusions which all succeeding aircraft designers used.

Rather later, in 1909, just down the road so to speak, a young man from Leeds named Robert Blackburn tried to fly from the beach at Marske-by-the-Sea in an aircraft of his own design. By 1914, Blackburn had established a base at Brough on the north bank of the Humber for marine aircraft...

Another attempt at flying took place on Beverley Westwood on 1 September 1910 when Gordon Armstrong, a local garage owner, tried to take off in a Blériot-type monoplane but was injured in the process and the exercise was abandoned. For many years afterward the aircraft could be seen suspended from the roof of the garage in North Bar Within.

With such a strong local heritage in aviation matters, it is hardly surprising that Harold Dalton Boultbee, who was born in Yorkshire in 1890, the son of the Reverend H.T. Boultbee, should show interest in such matters. Educated at Richmond School, and Queen's College, Cambridge, as early as 1909 he attempted to patent a design for a retractable undercarriage for an aircraft he and an associate were trying to build. This was never finished due to lack of funds.

In 1911 Boultbee joined the British and Colonial Aircraft Company (later the Bristol Aeroplane Company) at Filton, Bristol, as Chief Draughtsman. He left Bristol in 1915 for a brief stay with the Gloucestershire Aircraft Company before joining the Lincoln-based company, Ruston Proctor, as works manager. There he was responsible for producing licence-built B.E.2s and Sopwith Camels and Snipes.

Following the end of World War I, Boultbee returned to Gloucester as a member of the design team responsible for the Mars racing biplanes. There was then an unexplained hiatus in his career between 1921 until 1923 when Boultbee joined

Handley Page as Assistant Chief Designer to George Volkert.

At Handley Page, Boultbee quickly proved his ability by taking over the design of the HP Sayers Motor Glider. Three of these machines were produced: numbers 22,23 and 25. Drastic modifications introduced by Boultbee on number 25 meant that it was the only one of the trio to fly.

In 1924 Boultbee put forward a proposal for a light two-seat high-wing monoplane intended for entry into the Air Ministry's light Aeroplane Competition at Lympne that year. Lack of finance, however, prevented it being built.

The following two years saw Boultbee make what was probably his most significant contribution to aircraft design to date when he produced the preliminary drawings for the Handley Page Harrow biplane two-seat torpedo bomber. Although ultimately unsuccessful (it lost out to the Yorkshire-produced Blackburn Ripon) it produced a great deal of useful data pertaining to wing slots.

In December 1926 Boultbee began work on the Hare high-altitude bomber biplane, designed especially for easy maintenance in the field. Following a series of tests which were plagued by engine and vibration problems, Boultbee then designed a new undercarriage to suit the aircraft for a proposed new role as a land-based torpedo-bomber. Ultimately, the Hare never entered military service as better competing designs always seemed to appear at inconvenient times when the Hare was grounded with one problem or another.

Finally, in 1927, Boultbee began initial design work on what was probably his most successful type, the Handley Page Heyford heavy bomber. A large twin-engined biplane, its most interesting feature was the fact that the lower wing was close to the ground and carried the undercarriage and bombs to ease loading, while the upper wing with two engines and fuselage towered above it. Despite its rather odd appearance, the Heyford proved to be surprisingly effective in use with the RAF and remained in front-line service until 1939.

Earlier, in 1926, the de Havilland Moth had been adopted as a trainer for several Air Ministry-approved flying clubs. Handley Page apprentice A.P. Hunt was the first of ten pupils to learn to fly in the traditional little open-cockpit two-seat biplane. In a conversation with Boultbee he remarked how cold the cockpits were in winter. This seems to have been the catalyst for Boultbee's decision to start design work on his ideal light aeroplane, a far more sophisticated concept than the Moth. For the next two years, Boultbee, assisted by Hunt, worked at home in the evenings to produce a complete set of drawings for the project. Finally, in 1928, both men resigned from Handley Page Ltd in order to build their prototype at Burton-on-Trent, forming a new company which they called

The Civilian Coupé

The Coupé was far from traditional for it was the first enclosed-cabin two-seat monoplane in Britain. As such it was the precursor to many of the light aircraft flying today which still adhere to its basic layout. At the time of the Coupé's debut, Boultbee and his associates had great confidence that the modernity of the aircraft would ensure its success; a confidence reflected in the Company's advertisements of the time:

"You, the pilot of experience and you, the complete novice, will I believe, alike find in the Civilian Coupé an aircraft to your needs. Experience as a designer has taught me how fatally easy it is to sacrifice one good quality for another, controllability to performance, comfort to view, ruggedness of structure to low weight. In the design of the Civilian Coupé I determined there would be no single point which the critic could select as having been neglected. You the user cannot know of the long process of elimination and repeated compromise which is necessary before so ambitious an aim is achieved.

But you can, and I hope will, by study of the specification and by actual flight trials, satisfy yourself that the Civilian Coupé has fulfilled the object that inspired its design, and justified our claim that it is the most practical light aircraft in existence today."

On 25 July 1929, the *Burton Observer* reported on the first aircraft to be completed:

**FIRST BURTON MADE PLANE
BID TO SUPPLY THE PRIVATE OWNER**

On Thursday in the yard of Messrs. S. Briggs & Co's Moor Street premises, a small group of people associated with the venue inspected the first Aeroplane produced by the Company and on Friday it left Burton to go to Heston Air Park, Hounslow, London, where it is to be exhibited as an example of the type of machine Burton can offer to private purchasers.

Heston Park is the demonstration ground for the Aero Show and it was thought advisable to show the machine there rather than at the show itself as it was the only one completed. It will take its first flight from Bass & Co's meadow in two weeks time.

The new company is known as the Civilian Aircraft Co., and its machine is the "CIVILIAN" Coupé. The Company has been formed as its name suggests to meet the rapidly developing private demand. Special regard is therefore being paid to comfort, convenience and ease of control.

The Company, which consists of Messrs W.B. Briggs, J.R. Shercliff, S.H. Buxton and T.S. Green with Mr H.D. Boultbee AFRAeS as Managing Director and

3: *Looking rather incongruous against the dismal industrial surroundings of the brewery yard, this is the prototype Coupé Mk I in late July 1929 before its maiden flight. Oddly, there seems to be no record of what colours it was finished in, although the fuselage may be in a clear varnish.*

4: *A view into the cockpit of G-AAIL through the open door, which in 1929 was a very great novelty indeed. The finishes and instruments are not unlike those of a sports car of the period.*

5: *A general arrangement drawing of the Civilian Coupé. Were it not for the angular fin and rudder, the aircraft would not be dissimilar to those designed ten years later. Perhaps a more elegant tail unit might have made it look faster and more glamorous...*

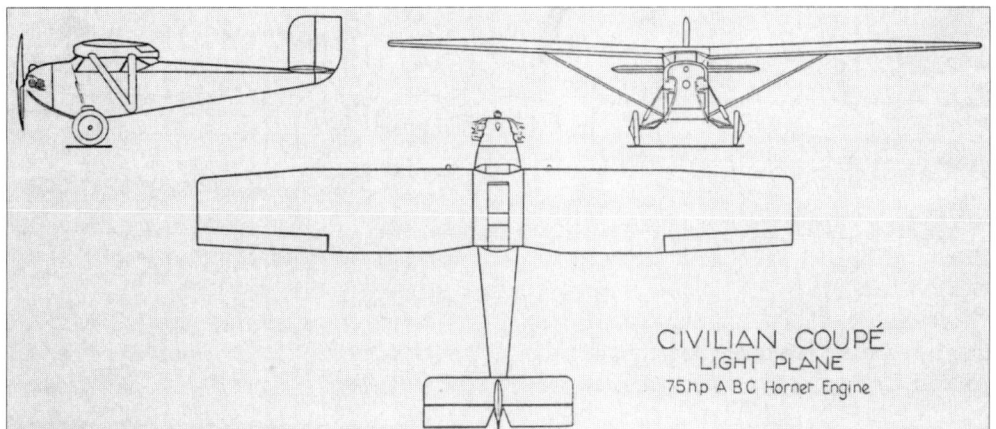

CIVILIAN COUPÉ
LIGHT PLANE
75hp A B C Horner Engine

6: This head-on view of G-AAIL shows off its clean and modern lines to advantage. The only real giveaway to its age is the undercarriage and its bulky rubber shock absorbers and the narrow tread tyres. Later aircraft tended to make more use of 'doughnut' tyres, although saving weight may have been a consideration for the designer. Suitable engines seem to have been Boultbee's biggest problem.

7: When making its first public appearance at Heston in July 1929, the Coupé was clearly from another generation.

8: Surrounded by conventional biplanes at Heston in July 1929, the Coupé looks what it was — a harbinger of the future. If it had not been for the Wall Street crash the year the Coupé was born, what might have become of the Civilian Aircraft Company?

9: Problems with the Coupé were remarkably few, but one particular difficulty was the engine and forward vision. This appears to be an attempt to improve both. It seems that the ABC Hornet motor has been retained. An extra fairing has been fitted on the undercarriage leg and the rudder chord appears to have been increased.

Mr A.D. Hunt ARAeS as Acting Works Manager, is announced as a new name with 20 years experience behind it.

This claim refers to the record of Mr Boultbee who is the son of the Rev. H.T. Boultbee, a former vicar of Holy Trinity Church, who has been constructing aircraft since 1909 and had a great deal of experience during the war, constructing large machines for high power and high altitudes.

Mr A.P. Hunt has also had a varied experience in the aircraft trade with which he has been connected since 1914, having been with the Handley Page Company. He accompanied the Prince of Wales when he made his first flight in a Handley Page Bomber over London.

The new Coupé is the product of two and a half months work by a complement of eight skilled men. It is a semi-cantilever monoplane and this is said to give the best arrangement for view and ease of folding and has the additional advantage of easing fuelling up.

The 3-ply covering adopted throughout results in a very strong weatherproof structure which will stand hard wear and is easy to repair; ball bearings are fitted to all control members, especially at points which may be overlooked or neglected.

The windscreens are arranged to give maximum visibility, including a good view to the rear when tail-down on the ground. There are easily detachable wide entrance doors on each side and a low chassis is a definite advantage when climbing in onto the seat cushion.

The construction throughout is on very robust lines with generously sized bolts.

An ABC 'Hornet' engine is fitted. This four-cylinder engine is rated at 75 hp. At 1,875 rpm it has a very low petrol consumption, it gives an excellent view over the nose of the machine and runs with an entire absence of vibration.

The unit is mounted on a steel tubular framework and includes the fireproof bulkhead, oil tank, instrument panel, all engine controls, oil pipes, filter and exhaust pipes.

WING SPAN: 35' 6" folding to 23'
LENGTH: 19' folding to 11'
TOTAL WEIGHT: 1,500 lbs
SPEED: 100 mph
CLIMB: 5,000 ft in 10 mins and 10,000 ft in 25 mins

The first flight took place on Sunday 11 August 1929 watched by one of the junior clerks of Briggs & Co (where the prototype was built), Eric Boyce, and his brother, Charles. Charles Boyce recalled many years later:

"My brother came home from the office one Saturday mid-day and said that the 'plane which was being built in Briggs's workshops was being taken to Bass's meadow (between two branches of the River Trent) on the Sunday morning for taxi-trials.

We got up earlier than usual and cycled to the meadows (which were used for grazing Shire horses used in the brewery) and the 'plane arrived with the tail being pushed on a handcart.

After awaiting around for a considerable time, someone (apparently a test pilot) got into the machine, had the engine started by swinging the propeller, and taxied around the meadow until, starting at the northern end, he came roaring up the field and became airborne, apparently to the surprise of those concerned.

He flew along the River Trent in a southerly direction, turned northwards over adjacent hills and touched down near to where he had started. By now it was Sunday dinner-time and we departed."

The flight was also witnessed by a reporter who wrote in the *Burton Daily Mail* the following day:

BURTON 'PLANE FLIES
Satisfactory Preliminary Tests
Ground trials of the Burton-built Civilian Coupé aeroplane of the Civilian Aircraft Co. were carried out at Bass's meadows early yesterday morning.

The 'plane, with folded wings, was pushed from the Moor Street Works to the flying ground shortly after dawn. Engine tests were made and Mr A.J. Sutcliffe, of the Midland Aero Club, taxied the machine across the meadow. He gathered speed and rather unexpectedly rose into the air. After a flight of about eight minutes he returned and made a perfect landing.

No further flying tests were carried out because of the high wind that was steadily gathering and it was thought desirable to take no risks with an experimental machine. Further tests will be made at the end of the week.The machine was found quite satisfactory and there was an entire absence of vibration or similar troubles.

The pilot went up in ordinary clothes without flying helmet or goggles and he declared he was perfectly comfortable.

Despite the optimistic claims, however, all was not perfect with the Coupé. It is interesting to compare this report with the words of the pilot concerned, W. H. Sutcliffe, chief instructor of the Midlands Aero Club, who the maiden flight:

"During this flight I found the machine flew quite well, but there was a lack of aileron control, and the flight was shortened by the hinged roof over the cockpit lifting, due to the tension in the clip springs being inadequate. Necessary alterations were subsequently made to the ailerons to make them more effective."

Sutcliffe also noted that:

"On take-off the machine required a considerable amount of right rudder in order to prevent swinging. When in the air the machine behaved perfectly on all controls. I stalled the machine several times and found the stalling speed was approximately 35 mph. After the machine had completely stalled the nose did not drop violently, and without easing the stick forward the machine regained flying speed very quickly. Very little rudder was required to prevent the machine spinning."

Additionally Sutcliffe found that:

"A slight forward load on the joystick was necessary with a passenger; a spring loaded device would be an advantage."

In two runs over a measured course the aircraft recorded a maximum speed of 96 mph at 2,080 rpm and 83.5 mph at 1,825 rpm. Climbing speed was noted as 60 mph.

Martlesham Heath

The Coupé, in its initial form, was recorded in Jane's *All the World's Aircraft* for 1929 as follows:

THE CIVILIAN AIRCRAFT COMPANY
OFFICE AND WORKS :27 MOOR STREET,
BURTON-ON-TRENT

The Civilian Aircraft Co., of Burton-on Trent, is one of the latest constructing companies to be formed in Great Britain. Its first product is a small tow-seat coupé monoplane, with the 75/85h.p. A.B.C. "Hornet" four-cylinder air-cooled horizontally opposed engine. The machine has many desireable features, including push and pull rod controls all mounted on ball-bearings, windows all round the cabin, including the back, giving a clear view between the wing and the fuselage, and a large door on each side of the cabin, allowing either occupant similar ease of access to their seats.

THE CIVILIAN "COUPÉ"

TYPE: *Single-engined high wing cabin monoplane*

WINGS: *Braced monoplane, of wooden construction. Wing structure consists of two box-spars of spruce and plywod, and a number of main ribs of similar construction. In between these ribs are located a number of intermediate former ribs. The whole wing is covered with plywood. The wings are carried above the upper fuselage longerons, the intervening space between the wing and fuselage be-ing filled with windows. One pair of Vees. The locking pins on the front spar-joints have a double safety catch.*

FUSELAGE: *Rectangular structure, of spruce longerons and stiffening struts with plywood cover.*

TAIL UNIT: *Monoplane type. Construction similar to that of the wings. The extremity of the fuselage, including the tail-plane, fin, rudder and tail-skid are built up as a complete unit and bolted to the fuselage by four bolts. All tail surfaces are cantilever.*

UNDERCARRIAGE: *Divided type. Each unit consists of a telescopic leg attached high up the side of the fuselage, the bottom end being hinged to the bottom fuselage longeron by a steel-tube Vee. All joints to the fuselage are by ball-joints enclosed in greaseproof leather stockings. Springing is by rubberblock in compression. A laminated leaf-sprung tail-skid is used.*

POWER PLANT: *One 75/85 h.p A.B.C. "Hornet" four-cylinder horizntally-opposed air-cooled engine. The engine mounting is a steel-tube unit which carries the engine, engine controls, and dashboard, with all necessary instruments. The main fuel tank, of 16 gallons capacity, is in the right-hand wing-root, giving gravity feed to the engine. Petroflex tubing at the rear spar hinge allows the wing to fold without disconnecting the fuel pipes.*

ACCOMMODATION: *Side-by-side seating in totally-enclosed cabin. Windows all round upper half of cabin. Two doors, one on either side. Dual control and wheel brakes will be fitted. A luggage locker is located behind the cabin, with an outside door on the left side of the fuselage.*

DIMENSIONS:
Span:	*36 ft 6 in (10.8 m)*
Length:	*19 ft (5.79 m)*
Width folded:	*11 ft 2 in(3.4 m)*
Length folded:	*23 ft (7.0 m)*

WEIGHTS:
Weight loaded (normal C. of A.): 1,500 lbs (680.4 kg)
Weight loaded (aerobatic C. of A.): 1,300 lbs (589.7 kg)

PERFORMANCE (estimated):
Maximum speed: 100 m.p.h. (160.9 km.h.)
Cruising speed: 83 m.p.h. (133.6 km.h.)
Stalling speed: 40 m.p.h. (64.4 Kkm.h.)
Climb to 5,000 ft (1,524 m.): 10 minutes
Climb to 10,000 ft (1,524 m.): 25 minutes
Service ceiling: 12,000 ft (3,660 m)

In this form, in September/October 1929 it was

sent for testing at the RAF establishment at Martlesham Heath in Suffolk which was then responsible for flight testing and certification of all aircraft in this country. There the Civilian Coupé fared none too well; the more professional Martlesham Heath pilots took a less charitable view of the handling of the aircraft. Both takeoff and landing characteristics were criticised, as was the forward view which was obscured by the ABC Hornet engine. Not only that, the notoriously bad surface of the Heath (there were no concrete runways in existence at this time) caused the undercarriage to collapse. Also, and more significantly, the vibrations caused five engine bearer breakages with the result that the engine was torn loose. In fact, weak engine bearers seem to have been the biggest single flaw of the Coupé.

A new Company

In the meantime, the premises at Moor Street had also been found to be unsatisfactory, for at some time during the summer of 1929 Boultbee moved the company to Horninglow Road North. Even this new location seems to have been regarded as temporary, as the Civilian Aircraft Company's entry in Jane's for 1930 noted. (See below). It also seems highly probable that as the delay in certification meant that aircraft could not be sold, with no income from sales the company was dangerously under-capitalised. Clearly, the company was going through a period of change, if not outright financial difficulties. As a consequence, negotiations must have started at about this time with Sir Benjamin Dawson, a recently-knighted Bradford mill-owner (made Baronet 2 July 1929) with interests in the woollen trade, with a view to new investment in the Civilian Aircraft Company.

Dawson's son, Lawrence, had made a start in the woollen business also but, after 18 months, had admitted that to his father that his heart was not in the woollen industry but in aviation. Consequently, the interests of both Boultbee and Dawson coincided, which eventually led to Dawson buying out Boultbee's co-directors (although A.P. Hunt was still connected with the company in mid-November 1930 when he signed off speed and altitude tests as the responsible pilot) and then appointing his son as managing director of a reformed Civilian Aircraft Company Limited. This new company was incorporated on 3 July 1930 specifically to produce the Civilian Coupé aircraft, wth a share capital of £25,000.

Return to Martlesham Heath

Following the trials at Martlesham Heath in autumn 1929, despite a bascally sound concept, there was a clear need for modifications to the Coupé to allow it to receive a Certificate of Airworthiness. These took time and it was not until June 1930 that the aircraft was ready for a second bout of trials. Jane's *All the World's Aircraft* for 1930 noted the changes, shown here in bold print:

THE CIVILIAN AIRCRAFT COMPANY LTD
OFFICE AND WORKS **(Temporary address)**
HORNINGLOW ROAD NORTH, BURTON-ON-TRENT

Directors: Sir Benjamin Dawson Bt, L.S. Dawson and H. D. Boultbee BA, AFRAeS

This Company was incorporated on July 3, 1930, and was formed to undertake the production of the Civilian "Coupé" which had been built and tested during the previous year by the Civilian Aircraft Co.

THE CIVILIAN "COUPÉ"

TYPE: Single-engined high wing cabin monoplane

WINGS: Braced monoplane, of wooden construction. Wing structure consists of two box-spars of spruce and plywod, and a number of main ribs of similar construction. In between these ribs are located a number of intermediate former ribs. The whole wing is covered with plywood. The wings are carried above the upper fuselage longerons, the intervening space between the wing and fuselage being filled with windows. One pair of Vees. The locking pins on the front spar-joints have a double safety catch.

*FUSELAGE: Rectangular structure, **in two sections, the forward part of steel tubes bolted together with simple joints and the after-section** of spruce longerons and stiffening struts with plywood cover.*

TAIL UNIT: Monoplane type. Construction similar to that of the wings. The extremity of the fuselage, including the tail-plane, fin, rudder and tail-skid are built up as a complete unit and bolted to the fuselage by four bolts. All tail surfaces are cantilever.

*UNDERCARRIAGE: Divided type. Each unit consists of a telescopic leg attached high up the side of the fuselage, the bottom end being hinged to the bottom fuselage longeron by a steel-tube Vee. All joints to the fuselage are by ball-joints enclosed in greaseproof leather stockings. Springing is by rubberblock in compression. **Wheel-brakes and a steerable tail wheel are fitted as standard.***

POWER PLANT: One 75/85 h.p A.B.C. "Hornet" four-cylinder horizntally-opposed air-cooled engine. The engine mounting is a steel-tube unit which carries the engine, engine controls, and dashboard, with all necessary instruments. The main fuel tank, of 16 gallons capacity, is in the right-hand wing-root, giving gravity feed to the engine. Petroflex tubing at the rear spar hinge allows the wing to fold without disconnecting the fuel pipes. **The 103-110 h.p. Armstrong Siddeley "Genet Major" five cylinder radial engine may be fitted if desired.**

ACCOMMODATION: Side-by-side seating in totally-enclosed cabin. Windows all round upper half of cabin. Two doors, one on either side. Dual control and wheel brakes will be fitted. A luggage locker is located behind the cabin, with an outside door on the left side of the fuselage.

DIMENSIONS:

Span:	36 ft 6 in (10.8 m)
Length:	19 ft (5.79 m)
Width folded:	11 ft 2 in (3.4 m)
Length folded:	23 ft 3 in (7.09 m)
Height:	**6 ft (1.83 m)**

WEIGHTS:
Weight empty: 918 lbs (416.7 kg)
Weight loaded (normal): 1,500 lbs (681 kg)
Weight loaded (aerobatic C. of A.): 1,300 lbs (590 kg)
Wing loading 9 lbs/sq ft (43.9 kg/m)
Power loading 20 lbs/h.p. (9.08 kg/h.p.)

PERFORMANCE (ABC "Hornet"):
Maximum speed: 102 m.p.h. (163.2 km.h.)
Cruising speed: 85 m.p.h. (136 km.h.)
Stalling speed: 36 m.p.h. (57.6 Kkm.h.)
Initial rate of climb: 550 ft/min (167.7 m./min)
Range at cruising speed (normal tank) 360 miles (576 km) or 4¹/₂ hours
Service ceiling: 16,000 ft (4,880 m)

PERFORMANCE ("Genet Major"):
Maximum speed: 116 m.p.h. (163.2 km.h.)
Cruising speed: 96 m.p.h. (153.6 km.h.)
Landing speed: 36 m.p.h. (57.6 Kkm.h.)
Initial rate of climb: 800 ft/min (244 m./min)
Range at cruising speed (normal tank) 360 miles (576 km) or 4¹/₂ hours
Service ceiling: 16,000 ft (4,880 m)

PRICE (Provisional): £650

With the new modifications completed, the Coupé prototype, G-AAIL, was returned to Martlesham Heath in June 1930. This time the response by the test pilots was much more positive:

"All controls are powerful and well harmonised. The view is very much improved and is now considered good for this class of enclosed-cockpit aero- plane. The take-off is quite good and control is quickly picked up. The aircraft is easy to land and there is very good control on all surfaces on the glide-in to land."

At the stall the Coupé's Goettingen 387 wing section gave innocuous handling, the report stating that:

"Control was regained quickly with a small loss of height."

And so the Civilian Coupé Mk I finally gained its Certificate of Airworthiness on 5 June 1930.

A pilot's view

By the end of 1930, the Coupé had obviously been test flown and favourably reviewed by pilots writing for the sport flying magazines of the time. The following article taken from the January 1931 issue of *Motor Sport* is a typical example:

A LIGHT CABIN MONOPLANE
The "Hornet-" engined Civilian Coupé.

When its development elsewhere is considered, the enclosed small aeroplane has been rather slow in materialising in this country, but now that it has been taken up seriously by our leading manufacturers it is safe to foretell that within the next few years it will be the prominent type.

The most obvious advantage of the cabin machine is that it affords a great increase in comfort to the occupants, making special kit unnecessary and conversation without the use of telephones possible. But apart from these features, the typical high-wing monoplane, when combined with the cabin arrangement, can be designed so as to give a particularly clean exterior with a consequent reduction in air resistance and drag and therefore a high performance; good visibility for the pilot can be arranged, and a normal and easy access and egress can also be provided by a door at the side of the fuselage — a palpable improvement on the clambering-up-and-squeezing-in business necessary with open cockpit machnes.

These points, are of course, apparent to everyone now but credit is due to Mr. H. Boultbee, the designer of the Civilian Coupé machine here described, for realising them as long ago as 1926, for it was then that this 'plane, which has only recently been placed on the market, was first evolved.

Incidentally, while the Civilian machine is a definite newcomer, it is interesting to recall that Mr. Boultbee has been associated with aviation for over twenty years and was for a considerable period connected with the Handley Page concern.

As can be seen from the accompanying illustra-

TELEGRAMS: "CIVILIAN. BURTON."

TELEPHONE No.: 978.

THE CIVILIAN AIRCRAFT CO. LTD.

DIRECTORS:
SIR BENJAMIN DAWSON, BART
LAWRENCE S. DAWSON.
H. D. BOULTBEE, B.A., A.F.R., A.C.S

Horninglow Road North,
Burton-on-Trent.

Nov: 17th., 1930.

ALTITUDE TEST NO. 1 - Date, November 11th., 1930.

Altitude	Engine Revs.	Time.	Remarks.
0	1,900	0	
500	"	2.35	Climbing at 52 m.p.h.
1,000	"	2.55	"
2,000	"	5.15	"
3,000	"	7.15	"
4,000	"	9.30	"
5,000	"	12.45	("
6,000	"	25.20	(Kept losing height.
7,000	"	40.	(-do- , also
8,000	(1,950 at 7200ft.		(air speed increased to
9,000	(1,975 "		(65 m.p.h., machine failing
10,000	"		(to climb at 52 m.p.h.

Maximum height reached:- 7,200 ft.

PILOT.

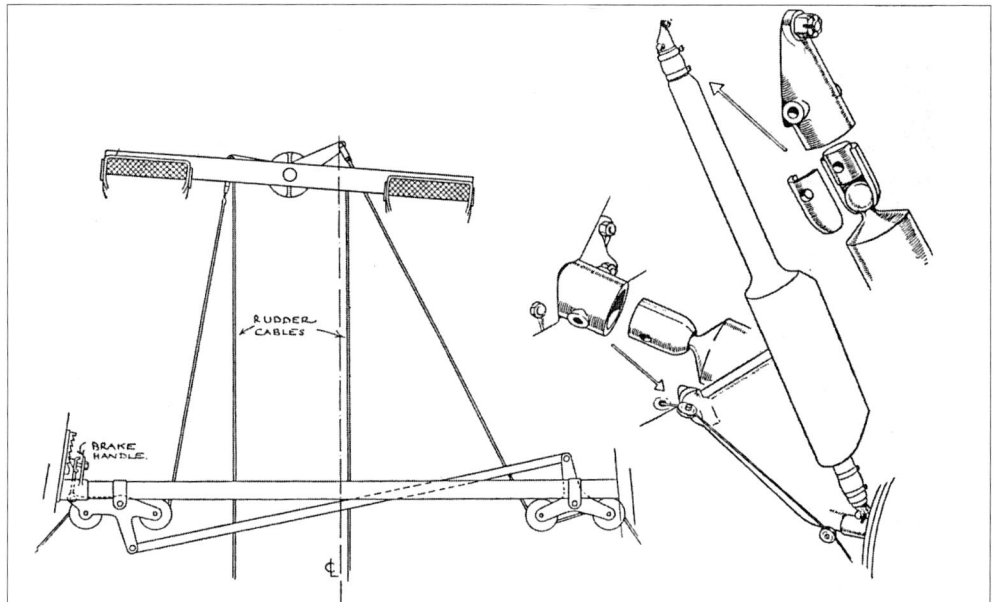

RUDDER CABLES

BRAKE HANDLE.

THE CIVILIAN COUPÉ

The First Enclosed Two Seater Monoplane in England
(DESIGNED 1926)

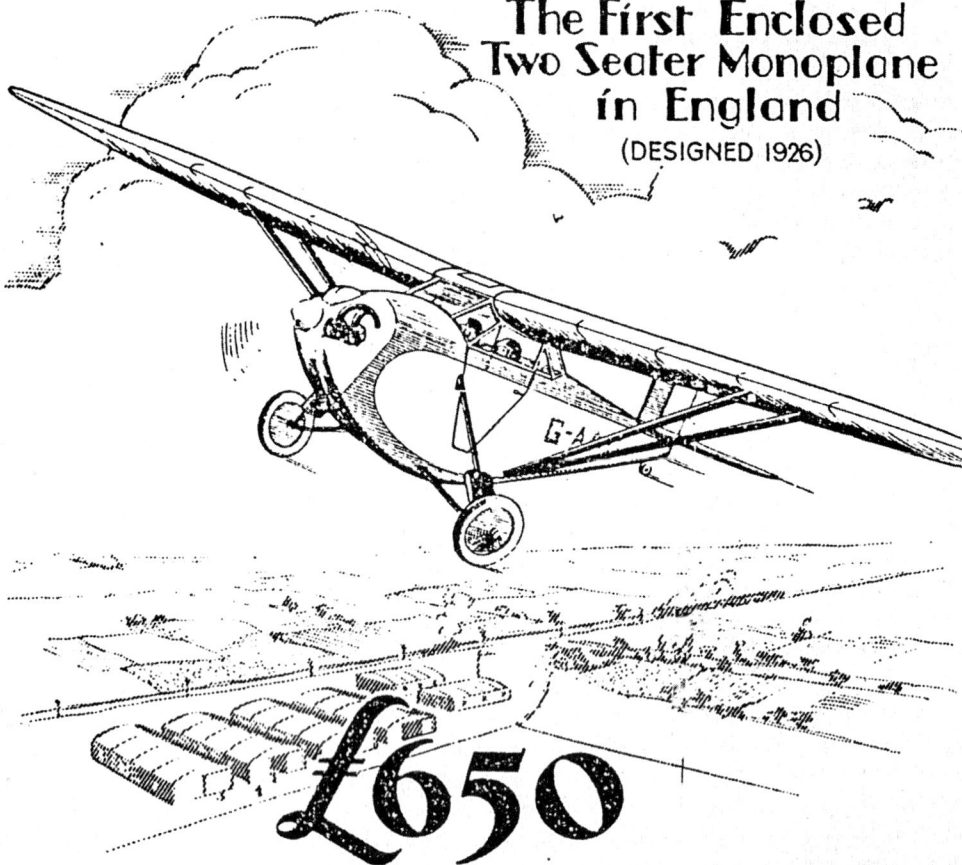

G-A...

£650

METAL CONSTRUCTION; 3-PLY COVERED 'PLANES; SOCIABLE SEATING; FINISHED AND TRIMMED LIKE A CAR; DUNLOP WHEEL BRAKES; FOLDING 'PLANES; OCCASIONAL 3rd SEAT.

THE CIVILIAN AIRCRAFT CO., BURTON-ON-TRENT.

12: A charming advertisement, typical of the period, showing the Coupé on offer at a bargain price. Note the reference to an 'occasional 3rd seat'. This particular feature never appeared; the aircraft was simply too small and under-powered.

13: The A.B.C. 'Hornet' 'flat four' engine which at first seemed to be a good choice of powerplant for the Coupé as it was relatively small in size, offering about 75 hp. Designed by the same company which had earlier produced the 'Dragonfly' engine, which had spectacularly failed to live up to its expectations at the end of World War I, it seems that the Hornet could also be rather temperamental. When the larger Coupé Mk II appeared, the Hornet had to be replaced by the larger Armstrong Siddeley 'Genet Major'.

tion, the Civilian is a monoplane with the mainplane braced by "V" lift struts. In construction it follows orthodox practice, incorporating spruce box spars and three-ply and spruce ribs. The wing section adopted is said to have a very high stalling angle, and the wing tips are tapered with the object of giving a large degree of lateral control. The convering is of three-ply, reinforced at the leading edge to prevent any deformation. The wings are made to fold, and are attached at their roots to the fuselage by simple but robust fittings; they are anchored to a steel tube structure which forms the top half of the cabin framework.

The folding procedure is particularly easy, and can be done single-handed without disturbing the lift struts or aileron control, No jury struts are necessary for supporting the wings when in the folded position, and the locking-pins on the front spar fittings have double safety catches.

The Fuselage

The fuselage is of composite construction, the rear part being built up in box girder fashion with spruce longerons and members and three-ply covering. The front section, which includes the cabin and engine mounting, is of steel tubes bolted together with simple joints. The interior of the rear end of the structure is readily accessible for inspection or attention through a detachable fairing.

The tail unit of the Civilian is very neat and clean in appearance, being devoid of all exterior bracing, cranks or king post. Both the elevator and fin are of full cantilever construction and the complete empennage, comprising rudder, fin, tailplane and elevator are secured to the fuselage by four bolts. As in the case of the main planes, the covering is of plywood.

The control mechanism is rather unusual; no cables are used, the connection between the stick and rudder bar to the various controlling surfaces being by pull-and -push rods. Ball-bearings and oilless bushes are used throughout, waste action is obviated. All control levers are concealed, giving unbroken surfaces to the tail and ailerouns.

The undercarriage, in keeping with modern ideas, is of the axle-less type, with a wide track (6 feet 6 inches). Landing shocks are take by rubber absorbers, in compression, and the whole arrangement of the components is covered by neat streamline fairing pieces. The top end of the legs are attached to the top longerons and the "V" radius rods pivot on ball joints, which are enclosed in grease covers, on the bottom members. The undercarriage is equipped as standard with Dunlop wheels fitted with Bendix brakes. These are operated independently for taxying, by the rudder bar or together by a convenient hand-lever. On the production models of the Civilian, a small wheel replaces the tail skid; this renders a trolley unnecessary when the machine is being moved about in the hangar, and at the same time, lessens the strains imposed on the fuselage in landings.

The cabin accommodates two people, the pilot's seat being on the port side. They are carefully designed to give a really restful position, and are fitted with air cushions. Removal of the passenger's seat leaves a space of 10 cubic feet, and quite large and bulky goods can be easily loaded through the wide side doors.

The furnishing of the cabin interior is well carried out the walls being covered with either hide or cloth. Handrails and a foot rest for the passenger are fitted as standard. The instruments are neatly arranged on a fascia board, and a locker is provided for maps. Besides the extra space made possible by removing the passenger seat, ample room is also available within the cabin to the rear of the pilot. Golf clubs, fishing tackle and the like can be housed in a locker beneath the fairing to the rear of the cockit. Naturally, all windows have safety glass, and one of the outstanding features of the machine is the exceptionally good view above, in front, at the sides and behind.

The Engine

The standard power unit installed in the Civilian is the well-known A.B.C. 75 h.p. "Hornet" flat four. It is supported on a steel tublular mountng, so arranged as to minimise any vibration being transmitted to the rest of the machine. The throttle and ignition controls, oil gauge, and revolution indicator are all conveniently grouped so as to simplify matters when the unit is taken out for overhaul, and the engine itslef is secured by four conveniently-situated bolts. A fireproof bulkhead is built into the nose, at the rear of the engine, and behind this is the oil tank.

Feed to the carburettor is by gravity, the fuel tank being situated in the port wing, near the root; it has a capacity of twenty gallons. This gives a range at cruising speed of about 360 miles (4 1/2 hours).

Under test the experimental machine, which was first built in 1929, shows good all round qualities with a top speed of 102 m.p.h. The rate of climb is 550 feet per minute, and its ceiling is about 16,000 feet.

The article was accompanied by two pictures of the Coupé prototype, G-AAIL, in flight. Very few such photos of this first aircraft are known.

In flying position. The Civilian Coupe monoplane. The production machines will differ in certain details from the one shown here ; the tail skid, for example, will be replaced be a small wheel, and the latest type Dunlop-cum-Bendix wheels will be incorporated.

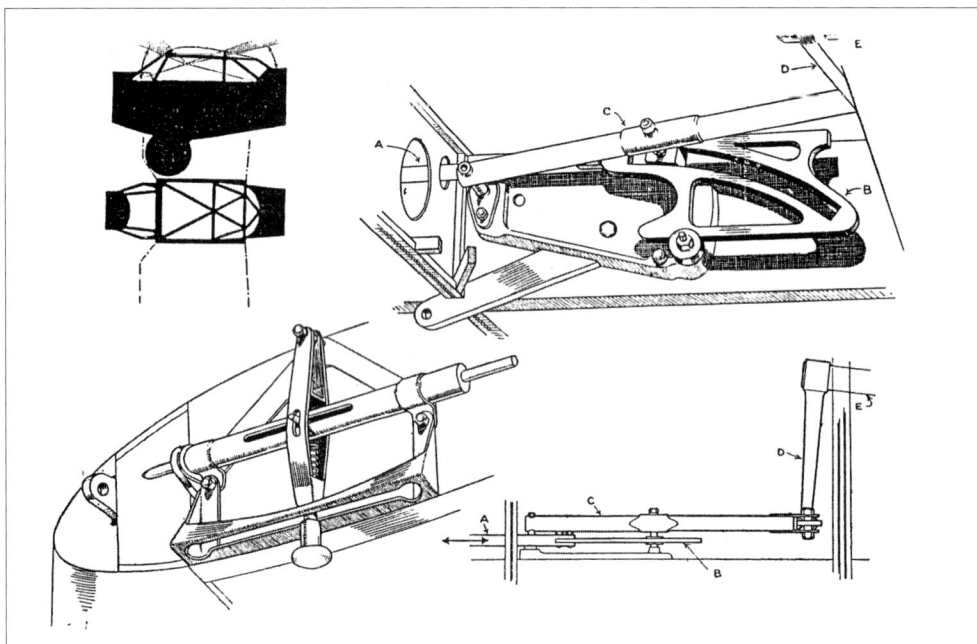

14: *A grainy copy of a picture featured in the review of the Coupé in the January 1931 issue of* Motor Sport, *noting the intended changes to the undercarriage on the production version of the aircraft.*

15: *More technical sketches from* Flight. *This time they show details of the wing-folding mechanism and the pushrod control system. This was a vast improvement over the cables and pulleys common in all other light aircraft of the period, the rigid rods and bearings being impervious to the stretching, wear and high levels of maintenance associated with the older system.*

16: *G-AAIL, seen here at Hedon on a typical airfield surface of the period. It still retains the Hornet engine, so is it possibly just before or just after the company had moved to Hedon, in January 1931. By March the prototype had been fitted with the Genet Major engine. Standing in front is G.R. Webster, one of the last employees of the Civilian Aircraft Company and who worked on the advanced three-engined aircraft project dreamed up by Harold Boultbee.*

17: *This partial test report by an unidentified pilot dating from September 1929 reveals that a number of weaknesses in the design of the Coupé have been attended to. These included the poor forward view, now made "entirely satisfactory". The note about landing behaviour may be a clue to the obvious difficulties which later beset inexperienced pilots. The RAF pilots at Martlesham Heath, initially lukewarm about the aircraft were later very positive after the modifications had been made.*

Flying Report.

Week Ending 12th September, 1929.

<u>Hours Flown</u>.   2.45   <u>By Self</u>:   1.15   <u>By R.A.F.</u>

<u>Machine</u>.   Civilian Coupe G.AAIL.

<u>Remarks</u>.

Machine took off with decided swing to left which was only checked by full opposite rudder.   Climbed well; and in the air could be controlled perfectly.

Machine has small turning circle and turns of varying 90° can be made with ease and machine recovers quickly.   Controls were very light and sensitive.

(The forward view is definitely bad and one cannot see ahead either on the ground or in the air). *This has since been made entirely satisfactory*

Throttle position is perhaps to the average person in an awkward position, all instruments are easy to read and in an excellent position, ~~the~~ ^No^ draught penetrated cabin either with sides open or closed.

Engine has no vibration; runs well; Exhaust is very noisy *(modified)* making speech difficult.

Machine will not fall into a violent stall and can be flown with stick hard back and engine throttled back, in this position application of rudder causes wing to drop, but this can be picked up by opposite aileron.   The wing section seems to be ideal for slow flying more so than other machine I know whether with slots or not .

Landing,at first Machine is tricky to land owing to very sensitive controls; floats in a long way and will finally sink down very slowly at an estimated speed of 30 to 35 M.P.H.

Landing, faster machine lands much easier.   There is great marked control over machine when machine is taxying, it can turn ^way^ either at 40 M.P.H. without the slightest tendency to turn up or dip a wing.   After landing machine pulls up quickly.

Consolidated Reports by R.A.F. Test Flight Two pilots, are: Machine takes off and lands very well. Machine is most pleasant in

CHALLENGING EXPERT OPINION !

Experts have said that it will be many years before all the refinements of modern light aeroplane design can be incorporated in a reasonably-priced aircraft. The Civilian Aircraft Company now challenges this belief! · In the new Civilian Coupé, selling at £650, are such refinements as side-by-side seating; a warm enclosed cabin with perfect all-round view; wings that fold without jury struts or disconnection of the controls; wide doors giving easy entrance and egress; low fuselage; complete elimination of fabric, of rigging and adjustment points. With this goes fool-proof control, and a maximum speed of 106 m.p.h. with the 75 h.p. model, and 120 m.p.h. with the 105 h.p. model.

Four years ago the first Civilian Coupé was built, planned by a designer of 21 years' experience. Since then every detail of its design has undergone rigorous practical scrutiny. Now, at last, those responsible for the Civilian Coupé are satisfied. In the carefully planned works at Hull Airport the first Civilian Coupés for sale to the public are being completed.

For full details write to :

CIVILIAN AIRCRAFT CO. LTD.,
AIRPORT OF HULL
HEDON - - YORKS

CIVILIAN COUPÉ

Save time by using the Air Mail.

xxi

18: *The confident tone of this advertisement from Flight of 10 April 1931 came at a time when the future for the Civilian Aircraft Company looked very bright. But hard times have no favourites and the Depression was to play a terminal role in the company's fortunes.*

19: *G-ABNT, the third Mk II, at Hedon in 1931 in company with the Hull Aero Club's De Havilland Puss Moth, the first example of which had flown about a month after the Civilian Coupé. The Puss Moth was the more successful design for with the resources of the De Havilland company behind it over two hundred and sixty were built. From the beginning it was fitted with an engine of more than twice the power of the Coupé, and was used on numerous record-breaking flights, several by Amy Johnson and her husband. Possibly engine choice was the biggest error made by Harold Boultbee in his design. Note the LNER railway line in the background and the garage-style aircraft fuel pumps. During airshows and, in earlier times, during race meetings, there was an unmanned railway halt ('Hedon Halt') for the use of passengers.*

Less than a month after the new directors took control, the first approach was made to the Hull Corporation with a view to the Civilian Aircraft Company leasing or buying Corporation-owned land on the site of what was then known as the Aerodrome, some five miles east of Hull at Hedon.

Originally it appears that the plan was for the Civilian Aircraft Company to move to an airfield close to Burton-on-Trent, both Burnaston or Brauston, in Leicestershire, apparently being considered. Neither was, however, in a completed state. Over at Hull, meanwhile, the Corporation had begun work on creating the first municipal airport in the country.

Minutes of the Hull Corporation's Aerodrome Committee dated 25 August 1930 record that Mr Dawson of the Civilian Aircraft Company had visited Hull that month and inspected that portion of the Aerodrome site (some 78 acres) which was not already leased to National Flying Services Ltd, the progenitor of the Hull Aero Club.

Hedon's attractions to both Dawson and Boultbee must have been several:
• The local council was wholeheartedly in favour of aeronautical development in the area *viz* the Aerodrome.
• Paull was earmarked as a seaplane base, leased from the War Office. At the time marine aircraft were seen as the major type envisioned for use on long-range civilian air transport routes, as a result there were potential opportunities for design and production of both land and marine aircraft types.
• Blackburn Aircraft were already established in the area, there was therefore a pool of locally skilled

labour already available and, perhaps not least in importance, both Dawson and Boultbee were native Yorkshiremen.

On 27 August, Sir Benjamin Dawson and his son visited Hedon again and met the Aerodrome Committee, which led to an initial offer of a seven-year lease at a rental of £100 per annum. By 15 October, however, the Committee had clearly had second thoughts, for the proposed rental now was to be £150 per annum for 14 years. The Civilian Aircraft Company's response is not recorded, although the first objections to the position of the airfield had been received from British Industrial Solvents at Saltend, south of the airfield site on the bank of the River Humber. The company was concerned about aircraft flying low over their factory. A note was sent from the Aerodrome Committe to National Flying Services regarding such practices.

At the same meeting it was resolved that the airfield be henceforth known as the 'Hull Municipal Aerodrome'.

By January 1931, Hull Corporation was expending a great deal of effort in promoting the Aerodrome, with numerous plans for its development, including better facilities for visitors and a sustained advertising campaign in *Flight*. The question of premises and a lease for the Civilian Aircraft Company had not, apparently, been settled for the company had written to the Council stating that they were not prepared to continue negotiations, although the matter might be revived in the future.

Notwithstanding the absence of a signed legal agreement between Hull Corporation and the company, the decision to move to Hedon had already been made, for a sticker placed on company purchase order number 374, issued on 20 January 1931, noted that with effect from 31 January the new address of the Civilian Aircraft Co. Ltd would be at the "Airport of Hull, Hedon, East Yorks". The new location was a long brick building on the north side of Hedon Road, almost directly opposite British Industrial Solvents, now known and used today as the 'Airport Garage'.

By March hopes were running high for the future of the Civilian Aircraft Company, when an article in the *Hull Daily Mail* of Monday 2 March revealed the existence of a Genet-powered aircraft at Hedon:

HULL FACTORY TO MAKE ONE 'PLANE PER WEEK

There were many admiring eyes directed at an attractive-looking aeroplane at the Hull Municipal Aerodrome on Saturday, and much surprise was occasioned when it leaked out that it was the first machine produced by the new Civilian Aircraft works which adjoins the aerodrome, and is situated on land leased to the company by the Hull Corporation.

The 'plane, which is a two-seater coupe, promises quickly to gain the forefront in the light aeroplane world.

It is fitted with a 110 h.p. "Genet" major (sic) engine, and as I discovered during a trip with Capt. Pennington on Saturday, has a top speed of something approaching 130 miles an hour, with a stalling speed of 40 miles an hour.

The side by side seating accommodation is unusually comfortable, and being completely enclosed the noise of the engine is sufficiently muffled to allow conversation between pilot and passenger to be carried on quite easily.

Mr H.D. Boultbee, the designer of the machine received quite a number of congratulations, among them being Councillor Frederick Till, the chairman of the Hull Development Committee, whose daughter was taken for a flight by Capt. Pennington.

It is estimated that the factory will turn out at least one 'plane per week.

As no other Coupé aircraft received a Certificate of Airworthiness before 14 April 1931, it is apparent that the prototype, G-AAIL, must have been fitted with the Genet engine at this time. It probably kept this engine until it was sold in April 1933 to Mr T. E. Richardson, the then flying instructor and later chairman of the Hull Aero Club.

The promised revival in negotiations between Hull Corporation and the company concerning the lease must have taken place remarkably quickly, however, when the *Hull Daily Mail* for 1 April reported in glowing terms on the rollout of the first production example:

'PLANE MADE IN HULL
Christening Ceremony at Hedon
PRODUCTION INCREASED

There was a pleasing ceremony at the Hull Municipal Aerodrome at Hedon, yesterday, when the first light aeroplane produced by the new Civilian Aircraft Company which has its factory on the edge of the aerodrome, was christened. The ceremony was performed by Lady Dawson, the wife of Sir Benjamin Dawson, Bart, who is a director of the company, and whose son, Mr Lawrence S. Dawson, is the live personality in the actual running of the factory. Lady Dawson said that although she was not a flying woman she was proud to have the honour of christening the new machine. She wished it every success on its journeys, and the Civilian Aircraft Company prosperity.

NEW ERA FOR OWNER PILOTS

Later in the club house Councillor F. Till joined in wishing the new company prosperity. Mr. Dawson had been working morning, noon and night, and he was quite sure that he was going to make the company a very real success. In Hull they had some great advantages from the point of view of flying, and he believed that the city which possessed a magnificent aerodrome was going to go ahead in the world of aviation. Before long they would probably have air services to the Continent, and they wanted to make Hull a real air-port and a real flying city. He expressed pleasure at the establishment of the factory at Hedon, and congratulated those responsible for producing a light 'plane "which heralded a new dawn for the owner pilot." Many of them for a comparatively small sum — about the cost of a motor car — could become the owners of the new 'Civilian Coupé'. There were many practical advantages in having their own 'planes, and he understood it was hardly more difficult to learn to master a light aeroplane than to handle a car.

TRIBUTE TO DESIGNER

Sir Benjamin Dawson, replying, said he wished every aeroplane — not only those produced by his own company — every success. He paid a tribute to the designer, Mr. H.D. Boultbee, who, he said, had evolved a machine which was a credit to the company and likely to be very popular. He mentioned that his son had first entered his own textile business and although he had worked hard for eighteen months without complaint he eventually indicated that his heart was not in the business and that he must go in for aeroplanes. "I believe he hated the sight of wool," remarked Sir Benjamin. "Eventually we found Mr. Boultbee and joined up with him, and that is why we are here today manufacturing aeroplanes."

The new 'plane, as announced in the 'Mail' some weeks ago, is an attractive looking coupe with side-by-side seating and comfortable appointments. It has had a thorough test at the hands of men of experience before being put on the market, and the finished article has come in for great praise. Fitted with either a 75 h.p. Hornet engine or a 105 h.p. Genet Major, it has a remarkable performance to its credit, and has already earned the reputation for being almost "to fly itself". It is certainly easy to handle, and fitted with the larger engine has a top speed of 110 miles per hour, a figure which we easily exceeded when a 'Mail' reporter had a trial trip the other day. The machine has been splendidly received by the trade and orders have already been handed in. As has been mentioned previously, it is anticipated that at first, the factory will be able to turn out about one a day.

The Coupé Mk II

Troubles with the ABC Hornet engine in the prototype, mostly to do with lack of power output, led to the decision to install the 100hp Armstrong Siddeley Genet Major I radial engine into the improved Mk II version of the Coupé. This offered better reliability and performance, particularly in regard to maximum speed and altitude. A subtle modification was the slight staggering of the seats so that the passenger had slightly more elbow room.

By the summer of 1931, production of the Civilian Coupé II was getting underway in earnest, with the first aircraft, number 0.2.1, registered as G-ABFI, being followed by 0.2.2, G-ABFJ. For unknown reasons, the second aircraft was granted a Certificate of Airworthiness ('C of A') before its predecessor on14 April 1931, 'FI not receiving permission to fly until 9 June.

It seems that at its peak the Civilian Aircraft Company Ltd had over fifty employees.

While the main construction of the aircraft was obviously carried out by the Civilian company, it appears that final painting and finishing was sub-contracted to a Hull coachbuilding (?) firm, H. Moses and Sons Ltd, for various purchase orders to that company specify upholstering, trimming, painting and lettering.

For example, order 622, dated 27 March requires upholstering to G-ABFI, and a carpet and retrimming of the cabin to G-ABGJ. On 17 April, order 708 specifies 'painting and lettering to G-ABFI', while order 780 of 4 May requires repainting to parts of G-ABFJ. More specifically, order 925 of 2 July confirms 'painting in blue and aluminium - one Civilian Coupé, G-ABNT'. This was the third Mk II, construction number 0.2.3, which was not registered until 10 September 1931.

Racing Coupés

In the 'twenties and 'thirties, it was the custom for the qualities of light civilian aircraft in particular to be judged by their racing performance. This quite illogical practice took little notice of economy, longevity, comfort or ease of maintenance for the private owner, factors for which the Coupé had been specifically designed. Nonetheless, Civilian aircraft therefore found their way into the racing game when G-ABFI earned quite a creditable seventh place at 119.4 mph in the London Heston-Newcastle Race on 30 May, flown by I.W. Mackenzie.

Despite not being officially granted a C of A until 9 June, G-ABFJ apparently also took part in this race, but did not finish, being obliged to force land after running out of fuel. It was probably being flown on a temporary registration as the pilot was G.A. Pennington, almost certainly the same Captain Pennington who featured in the *Hull Daily Mail* reports noted earlier. In the absence of contrary evidence, this suggests that he was serving as a company test or check pilot.

Nothing daunted, in June RAF Flt Lt V.S. Bowling bought 'FJ with the intention of flying it in the 1931 King's Cup Race to be held on the 25th of July.

Both machines were subsequently entered into the Hanworth-Blackpool race of 8 July 1931. Both, however, suffered engine trouble and were force landed. G-ABFI, flown by Tommy Rose turned onto its back after encountering a horse and a hedge while so doing at Iver, Bucks. L. S. Dawson (the Civilian Aircraft Company's Managing Director) in 'FJ managed a nose stand at Sandbach in Cheshire. This was, perhaps, the first intimation that the Coupé was not going to be the lucky aircraft its designer hoped for.

Repairs to 'FJ were not, however, possible in time for the King's Cup Race and Flt Lt Bowling failed to make the starting line. G-ABFJ never flew again and was written off, probably being used for spare parts.

Bowling was still unlucky in the Heston-Cardiff race of 19 September in brand-new G-ABNT, when he crawled home in tenth place at 89 mph — but at least he finished. Possibly the engine was too new.

At about this time an article in a so-far unidentified newspaper appeared which featured an illustration of G-ABFJ in a general review of the type:

The Civilian Coupe is something quite new in the light plane class. This machine, a two-seat cabin high-wing monoplane, is produced by the Civilian Aircraft Company, of Burton on Trent — a newly formed company to develop this particular type.

It is built mainly of wood. The chief components — fuselage, wings and tail surfaces — are of plywood, so that no fabric is used on the machine.

It is quite an easy one to recognise from its general lines, which are very unusual, and hardly likely to be confused with any other cabin machine. The almost square tail is a specially outstanding feature to note.

The designer has taken great care in the matter of good visibility, ease of maintenance, economy of upkeep, comfort, and so on.

An interesting feature is the very slow speed at which it can be flown.

Even at 40 m.p.h. there is no loss of lateral or directional control.

The wings can be folded back when in the hangar — a most important point in the saving of space.

Although it cannot be seen in the illustration (not shown here) *there is a transparent panel in the centre section for upward view, and this panel can also be used as an emergency exit.*

Notice the V-shaped wing-bracing struts.

The engine is an Armstrong Siddeley Genet-Major.

This little aircraft is going to be put on the market at about the same price as an open cockpit two-seater light plane, so it is likely to be popular this summer and very much in evidence.

Keep yours eyes open for it.

The piece appears to have been written rather earlier than 1931 (note the reference to Burton on Trent) but then re-used with an illustration of, and a refrence to, the Genet-engined Mk II.

Death of an aircraft company

In normal times, the minor teething problems attached to the production of any new aircraft would probably have been overcome but the optimistic forecasts of an aircraft a day leaving the Civilian Aircraft factory were never to be realised.

Despite the many good qualities of the Coupé, it could not escape the economic realities of the time. The effects of the infamous Wall Street stockmarket crash of 1929 were being felt in England also; the country was in the grip of the 'Great Depression'. In these straitened circumstances a personal aircraft, no matter how desirable, was an expensive luxury.

Between September 1931 and August 1932, only one other Civilian aircraft was fully completed and registered. This was number 0.2.5. which was built against an order from Germany. Registered G-ABPW on 27 August 1932, it was delivered to its new German owner in October, when its British registration was cancelled by the British authorities. This was not the end of the story by any means, however, of which more later.

What happened to the previous aircraft on the production line, number 0.2.4, is a mystery. The most likely explanation is that it was completed but never registered and may have been stored disassembled.

Apart from noting the address at the Airport of Hull, Hedon, and naming the directors, the entry for the Civilian Aircraft Company in Jane's *All the World's Aircraft* for 1932 simply carried the terse comment:

This Company was incorporated on July 3 1930 and was formed to undertake the production of the Civilian "Coupé," which had been built and tested during the previous year by the Civilian Aircraft Co. This machine has been described and illustrated in previous editions of this annual.

During the past year, negotiations for the re-organisation of the Company have been initiated, but at the time of going to press had not been completed.

At some point in 1932, however, probably sometime in September, Sir Benjamin Dawson withdrew his backing for the company. His other business interests, namely the woollen mills, may well have also been under considerable financial pressure. In the circumstances he probably had little choice but to cut his losses.

Boultbee was not one to give up easily, however, and he re-opened the factory again in October that year, for a letter on the company letterhead (which still notes the three directors) dated 13 October and addressed to Mr G. R. Webster of Ings Road, Hull, enquires whether he is presently out of a job, and if not to call round as soon as possible. The letter is signed by H.D. Boultbee.

The Civilian Aircraft Company Ltd was apparently still in business, albeit with a much reduced work force. Boultbee, far from disheartened, had an ambitious plan to produce a unique three-engined passenger aircraft. This had a high cranked wing, a circular section fuselage, a retractable undercarriage and one engine above the centre section. According to Mr Webster, the wings were completed and load-tested. The strength of the structure was such as to astonish the Government inspector who checked the load to weight ratio. A model of the proposed aircraft is believed to still exist.

But Boultbee was swimming against the tide. Such an ambitious project needed major financial support and potential buyers with money and confidence in unorthodox aircraft designs. Such desirable qualities were in short supply in 1933.

A further letter from Boultbee addressed to Webster and dated 11 February 1933, does not list any directors. It was much more sombre in tone, for it was a reference to a prospective employer:

TO WHOM IT MAY CONCERN

R. Webster was employed here from March 1931 to July 1931 & later this year when the works were reopened was chosen out of a large number of previous employees for a vacancy. We have found him to be a conscientious & hard working lad with considerable skill at woodworking. We have no hesitation in strongly recommending him.

Although no newspaper reports have been found which give details, according to the memories of Vincent Lockey, a Withernsea pilot and engineer, who held a licence which permitted him to overhaul and carry out limited repairs on Civilian aircraft, the assets of the company were put up for auction. (Probably sometime in April, just after G-ABFJ was sold). There he:

"bought quite a lot of spare bits after the firm had closed down."

And with that the Civilian Aircraft Company Ltd faded into history and obscurity.

Post-mortem

Although some flying clubs and their members received a degree of financial support from the Government, membership declined by ten per cent in only three months between December 1931 and March 1932. It seems probable that this fact more than any other prevented the Civilian Aircraft Company from fulfilling its early promise. There may be another less obvious factor, namely that many of the record-breaking flights over the previous four years, including Hull native Amy Johnson's famous flight to Australia in May 1930, had been successfully carried out by various De Havilland, mostly biplane, types. Among these was a spectacular flight from London to Cape Town in November 1931 in a De Havilland Puss Moth, a very similar machine to the Civilian Coupé. Consequently, the De Havilland types were perceived as more glamorous than the Coupé. It may just be that, to use a modern analogy, the Coupé was having to attack a well-established brand leader at a

20: T.E. Richardson, the Hull Aero Club's Chief Instructor, bought G-AAIL after the Civilian Company went bankrupt. Here his children pose in front of the aircraft which is now fitted with the Genet Major engine.

time of economic downturn. Simply put, it was the right aircraft at the wrong time — it may have just arrived too late.

And what of the designer, whose disappointment at the collapse of his dreams must have been very great? According to those who knew him, it appears that Boultbee was a man of little humour. Obviously highly intelligent, he was probably too serious for his own good. According to Dennis Rhys, whose brother Glyn owned G-ABNT for many years, Boultbee did not react well to criticism; a case in point being Boultbee's reaction when Rhys discovered cracked plates in the steel front structure of the aircraft, which he felt was not strong enough. This character trait may have served to distance Boultbee from many potential supporters.

With his company bankrupted, Boultbee had little option but to seek further employment, which he found with the British Klemm Aeroplane Company at Hanworth, near London. There he was involved in re-designing the German Klemm 25 to British standards. This was essentially an all-plywood aircraft, like the Civilian Coupé. Most were powered by Pobjoy engines.

The works manager at that time was George Handasyde who, like Boultbee, was one of the aviation pioneers and had also seen his own company founder.

The 'Swallow', as the Klemm was redesignated, was a highly successful aircraft but by 1934 Boultbee had moved on. Whether this was on account of friction between himself and Handasyde, a desire to start aircraft design from basics again, a connection with Pobjoy or simply a result of the prevailing economic climate is not known, but by 1934 Boultbee had found new employment with Pobjoy Airmotors Ltd of Rochester.

Best known for their aero engines, Boultbee designed for Pobjoy a three-seat plywood monoplane with folding wings which utilised the company's 90 hp Niagara III engine. Known as the 'Pirate' the sole example built, registered G-ADEY, first flew on 25 June 1935, but it remained a unique aircraft. With the experience of the Civilian Coupé behind him, Boultbee must have been aware that the larger three-seat aircraft would have been under-powered.

That same month the company reorganised itself and acquired a licence to build the Short Scion. The poor performance of the Pirate (it spent just one hour and ten minutes in the air before being scrapped in 1936) and the fact that Oswald Short was one of the directors of the new company probably had some bearing on this decision.

Poor disillusioned Boultbee resigned from the Royal Aeronautical Society on 8 February 1937 and never had anything more to do with aviation, his considerable talent unrecognised. It is believed he concentrated his energies thereafter towards the design of motor cars and eventually died aged 81 on 7 August 1967 at Rolleston, Staffordshire.

EI-AAV

1) NATIONALITY & REGISTRATION MARKS

CERTIFICATE OF REGISTRATION NUMBER: 36

3) TYPE & DESCRIPTION OF AIRCRAFT: Civilian Coupé C.A.C. 2 Seater monoplane

4) CONSTRUCTORS SERIAL NUMBER: 1

5) CERTIFICATE OF AIRWORTHINESS NUMBER: 2538
— CATEGORY: Normal
— SUB-DIVISION: (Cd)

6) OWNERS FULL NAME: Joseph Gilmore,
ADDRESS: Baldonnel Co. Dublin.
NATIONALITY: Irish

Cancelled 24.1.49
Owner deceased

7) USUAL STATION OF AIRCRAFT: Baldonnel, Co. Dublin

8) DATE OF REGISTRATION: 11th May, 1935

REMARKS

21: *Very much a period piece, this is a copy of the original Irish Aircraft Register Book which notes the details of the only Civilian Coupé ever to appear there, namely G-AAIL, here re-registered as EI-AAV. Although Joe Gilmore was killed in a flying accident in Canada in 1945, the registration was not cancelled until 1949.*

THE CIVILIAN COUPÉ MK I
Number 1 / G-AAIL / EI-AAV

22 Above: *EI-AAV after rebuilding and shown in the Irish Air Corps hangar at Baldonnel, near Dublin. Clearly visible in the background is the original wing of G-AAIL, damaged after Joe Gilmore's first crash (in England while returning to Ireland after buying the aircraft) in 1933. Faintly visible on the right is the tailplane of an Irish Air Corps Bristol F2B, an aircraft which dated back to World War I.*
(Picture from C. Bruton via G. Flood archive)

* *This is certainly incorrect. It is most probable that Maher is confusing a later purchase of parts in 1935 from Vincent Lockey in Withernsea, who had effectively bought all remaining spares after the final collapse of Civilian in February 1933. Obtaining money and spares probably took until 1935, hence the delay before the aircraft was formally registered in Ireland.*

First of all the Coupés, the solitary Mk I, construction number 1, was first registered as G-AAIL at rollout in late June 1929. Following testing at Martlesham Heath, which required several changes, it did not receive a Certificate of Airworthiness until 5 June 1930. It was then used for promotional purposes, being test-flown by many reviewers, who by and large reported favourably upon its qualities.

As the company's advertising stressed that an improved model was being offered for sale, it is not surprising that the aircraft was not sold but remained in Civilian ownership until the firm's final collapse in 1933. At the ensuing 'fire sale' it was sold on 2 April to T.E. Richardson, the Hull Aero Club's Chief Instructor. It seems, however, that it was not to his liking for his logbook records that he sold it on (to Michael D. Hewellyn Scott of the Skegness and East Lincolnshire Aero Club) on 16 May 1933, having flown only 6½ hours in it. Scott, apparently, did not like it either and sold it again in August, almost certainly to Irish pilot Joe Gilmore. As the following narrative records, Gilmore crashed on his way home, the wreckage remaining in England. Consequently it was not until 1935 that it was recorded on the Irish register as EI-AAV. In the following extract taken from *Aviation Ireland* of January 1973, Johnny Maher recalled Gilmore and his new aircraft:

Joe was a civilian mechanic employed by the (Irish) Army Air Corps. He spent most of his spare time overhauling cars and working on aircraft belonging to the Irish Aero Club and several private owners in order to get cash to finance his flying career. He eventually got his 'A' Pilot's Licence. He then became ambitious to have his own aircraft.

He achieved this ambition in 1935* when he answered an advertisement which appeard in Flight *magazine and arranged to purchase a small high-wing monoplane that the designer, Harry Boultbee, had decided to sell along with a lot of spares. These included a spare fuselage, tail plane, rudder and several bits and spares. As far as I can remember the price for the whole lot was about £100.*

Joe, having collected the necessary cash, left for England. He collected the aircraft and having made himself familiar with it, took off for Dublin. However, due to approaching darkness and not being too sure of the general direction of Dublin, he landed on a disused aerodrome near Carlisle. He slept in the aircraft that night and next morning obtained three gallons of petrol from a local garage. Unfortunately, when he removed the filler cap from his tank, he left it on the muddy ground. When he replaced it he did not notice that the vent hole in the cap was blocked by the mud. There was just enough petrol to get the engine started, run up and take-off before the engine cut (due to the vent in the tank being blocked) and Joe wrapped Civilian Coupe No. 1 around his neck, but escaped unhurt. He collected all the bits and pieces, had them stored in a local farmhouse and returned to Dublin.

*Later**, the possibility of rebuilding the aircraft was discussed and, in view of the amount of spares that were available, we did not see any great difficulty. Joe had the remains of his kite shipped back to Baldonnel and after examination we decided to scrap the fuselage* and the tail plane as they were practically write-offs. With the help of Ted Hoctor, who was the guiding hand in its rebuilding, the aircraft gradually became whole again. There were very little drawings available and it was necessary to depart from recognised procedures, in order to get the job completed.*

In fitting the tail plane, for instance, it was being fitted with a positive angle of incidence and Boultbee sent word that the tail plane must be fitted with a negative angle. The mainplane strut attachment fittings were damaged beyond repair, so Joe had new castings made in the Hammond Lane Foundry. It took him about three weeks to file them down to correct size, After the wings were fitted it was thought that the main left strut did not look healthy enough. To prevent them parting company from the fuselage and converting the kite into a flapping-wing aircraft, it was decided to fit a heavy cable that went underneath the fuselage and up alongside the struts to the strut attachment fittings on the mainplanes, both sides. And then came the day when the aircraft was flyable again.

In the rebuilding of the aircraft several difficulties were encountered and frequent contact had to be made with Boultbee, the designer. On the test flight Ted Hoctor instructed Joe to take the aircraft up to a bit of a hill that was on the Aerodrome, fly off, get the kite up a few feet and see how it handled. If it wasn't OK he was to land again. Joe took off, continued climbing and stopped up for about three-quarters of an hour.

The aircraft was designed for brakes to be fitted. But the rebuilt job had no brakes. This, coupled with the fact that the tail plane was fitted at a negative angle of incidence, had a blanking effect on the rudder and it was found that it was practically impossible to manoeuvre the aircraft on the ground. This meant that Joe had to get out of the aircraft any time he wanted to turn, lift the tail around and head the aircraft in the required direction.

The only payment Boultbee would accept for his help during the rebuilding was an Irish Sweep ticket blessed by a Rabbi.

Joe spent all his spare time flying and taking his helpers for joy rides and also doing a bit of aerial photography. The aircraft had a four gallon petrol tank in the starboard main plane but Joe could never afford more than two gallons at any one time, and sometimes even less. This shortage of fuel resulted in his having to concentrate on left hand turns only, as any time he made a right hand turn, the engine would cut. He eventually cured this by fitting a fuel pump that really pumped.

On one of his evening jaunts, as he was taking off, an ancient Irish terrier, the property of the Air Corps photographer Paddy Cleary, ran across his take-off path. The terrier was struck by the propeller, resulting in breaking off about 10 inches off the tips of both blades. Joe managed to stop the aircraft without further damage but Cleary's terrier was minus his left ear and plus a scar on his skull. Joe wheeled the aircraft back to the hangar, removed the broken propeller, collected the two broken tips and brought them over to my house to get my advice on what to do with them. I advised him to burn them but he would not accept that. He considered that the propeller could be repaired by gluing the tips on again and covering them with thin brass sheeting, screwed and soldered.

Joe was told that the prop would fly to pieces as soon as he opened up his engine, but he ignored all advice and spent two whole nights repairing it. I must say he made a beautiful job. He balanced it, refitted it to the engine, did a runup and lost about 100 revs, due to the increased weight of the prop. He wheeled the aircraft out to the aerodrome and took off. At about 500 feet the propeller flew to bits. Joe was left with about two inches of jagged boss whirling round about two feet from his face and a vibrating engine trying to jump out of its mounting. The vibration was so bad that he had to stand up in the cockpit to hold the control stick. The engine would not switch off as the switch wire was broken due to the vibration.

He managed to land in a field near the aerodrome and, by the time I got to him, he had his aeroplane out on the main road. With the tail on his shoulders he was wheeling it up the main road back to the camp, quite unperturbed and wondering only where he was going to get another propeller. Two of the engine bearer bolts had sheared and one engine strut was broken. Another three minutes in the air and Joe would have been flying a glider.

*Joe got the aircraft going again. He borrowed an engine mount from someone in Liverpool***, bought a propeller and continued his flying, using his aircraft for photographic purposes. Ultimately he crashed somewhere up near Saggart and the aircraft remains were dumped in Watkins' sand pit. So ended the life of Civiian Coupe No.1.*

When Joe Gilmore left the Air Corps he joined BOAC and worked on the Mayo Composite. He operated between Montreal and Baltimore. It was during his stay there that he salvaged a Fairchild cabin aircraft from the ice, rebuilt and flew it in his spare time. Lamentably he was killed in 1945 flying this aircraft, when it iced up on a flight to Montreal and spun in. Neither he nor his aircraft were ever found.

Oddly enough, the Irish registration was not cancelled until 24 January 1949 when it was noted "owner deceased".

*Possibly replaced by that of 0.2.4.

**This is probably the incident mentioned by Glyn Rhys — see page 35.

23 Above: *Harri Boon, proud co-owner of a Coupé Mk II, poses in front of PH-BBC in September 1933 at his home airfield, Welschap, near Eindhoven in the Netherlands. The machine appears to be finished in silver overall.*

THE CIVILIAN COUPÉ MK II
Number 0.2.1. / G-ABFI / PH-BBC

The improved Coupé Mk II differed from the prototype in having a wider fuselage, with slightly staggered seats which offered more comfort for the passengers, a tailwheel and brakes and the 105 hp Genet Major engine as standard.

The first of the breed, and the first aircraft to be built at Hedon, was registered G-ABFI, and took part in the Heston-Newcastle air race on 30 May 1931, although it was not awarded a Certificate of Airworthiness until 9 June 1931. It had been undergoing painting and lettering as far back as April.

Flown by I.W. Mackenzie it achieved seventh place at a speed of 119.4 mph, which appeared to augur well for the future. In the Hanworth to Blackpool race of 8 July, however, fuel shortage obliged Flt Lt Tommy Rose, the pilot, to force land at Iver, Bucks. The aircraft was damaged when Rose was baulked by a hedge and a horse while landing and the machine ended up on its back. Consequently it spent some considerable time undergoing repairs, and it was still awaiting a buyer in 1933. By then, as has already been related, the Civilian Aircraft Company had ceased to exist and the remnants had apparently been obtained by Harold Boultbee.

One Friday in March, perhaps in response to the same advertisement in *Flight* which caught the Irishman Joe Gilmore's eye, two enthusiastic and wealthy Dutch amateur pilots, Messrs H.J.P. Boon and F.C. Bazelmans, who jointly owned the 'City Garage' and the local bus company in Eindhoven, telephoned Hedon and enquired whether an aircraft could fly over to Welschap, as the airfield at Eindhoven was then known, the following day. They had in mind buying a sports 'plane and if the Civilian Coupé fitted the bill they would buy it on the spot.

Such a request must have seemed heaven-sent to those in Hedon and by the next morning at 11.30 the English pilot, known only as Newman, had landed G-ABFI at Welschap.

The 'National Flying School' had only recently opened (on 1 March) at Welschap, so Boon and Bazelmans had engaged André Postmaa, the instructor, to test-fly the Coupé as neither of the pair had a pilot's licence at the time!

Postmaa flew over Eindhoven throughout the middle of the day and by evening the aircraft had been bought and paid for. How Newman got home is not recorded.

On 29 April Coupé 0.2.1 was registered in the records at 'PH-BBC', the last three letters standing for 'Boon/Bazelmans/City Garage'.

Harri Boon, meanwhile, was determined to obtain his licence and undertook intensive instruction

24: *A rare picture of two Coupés together. Here G-ABFI and G-ABFJ are about to take off from Heston on 30 May 1931 at the start of the London to Newcastle air race. G-ABFJ ran out of fuel and force landed but G-ABFI came a creditable 7th at an average speed of 119 mph.*

Nº. *204* /

NEDERLAND

MINISTERIE VAN ·WATERSTAAT

BEWIJS VAN INSCHRIJVING

Nationaliteits- en inschrijvingskenmerk: PH- *BBC*

1. Type en beschrijving: *Civilian Coupé, landvliegtuig, tweepersoons eendekker.*
   ~~Bestemming~~: *Klasse: Niet- verkeersluchtvaartuigen.*
2. Naam en woonplaats van den fabrikant: *Civilian Aircraft Company Ltd Hedon, Yorks*
3. Fabrieksnummer: *0.2.1.*
4. Naam en voornamen van den eigenaar: *N V Stadsverkeersdienst "Eindhoven."*
5. Woonplaats van den eigenaar: *Eindhoven, Bleekstraat 43 B.*
6. Nationaliteit van den eigenaar: *Nederlandsch*
7. Plaats, waar het luchtvaartuig thuisbehoort: *Eindhoven*

De ondergeteekende, gelet op de verklaring, dat het hierboven omschreven luchtvaartuig niet is ingeschreven in een anderen Staat, stelt vast, dat dit luchtvaartuig op *29 April* 19*33* is ingeschreven in het Nederlandsche luchtvaartuigregister, overeenkomstig de voorschriften van de Bijlage A van het Verdrag houdende regeling van de luchtvaart van 13 October 1919, van de Luchtvaartwet van 30 Juli 1926 en van de Regeling Toezicht Luchtvaart van 6 December 1928, dat het zal voeren het nationaliteits- en inschrijvingskenmerk PH- *BBC*, en dat het de Nederlandsche nationaliteit bezit.

'S-GRAVENHAGE, *29 April* 19*33*.
(Handteekening) *van der Heyden*

Het B v i is geldig tot 29 April 1936 A. R.

Ingetrokken, vernield op 9/1/35 by Bijdrecht

✓

Opmerkingen: ......

25: *A copy of the Dutch registration document for PH-BBC:*
"Netherlands Ministry of Roads and Waterways, Proof of Registry.
Registration letters: BBC
Type and description: Civilian Coupé, land aeroplane, two people, monoplane
Name and location of maker: Civilian Aircraft Company Ltd, Hedon, Yorks
Makers number: 0.2.1
Name and Christian name of owner: City Traffic Service Ltd 'Eindhoven'
Address of the owner: Eindhoven, Bleekstraat 43B
Nationality of the owner: Dutch
Location of the aircraft: Eindhoven"

Quoting various regulations it goes on to say:
"... that it shall carry the nationality and registration letters: PH-BBC and that it has Dutch nationality.
'S-Gravenhage 29 April 1933
Signed
van der Leiden

This CVI is valid to 29 April 1936
A final note adds:
Withdrawn, written off, 30 December 1934 near Mijndrecht."

26: *Harri Jan Paul Boon's pilot's licence, valid until 22 June 1940 and giving his date of birth as 19 March 1896.*

27: *Harri Boon and his navigator, J.H. von den Nahmer, in September 1933, at about the time of their departure from Welschap to Reims to take part in an aerial rally and tour of France known as the 'Bienvenue Aérienne'. Forty aircraft took part in the event: 22 British, 9 Belgian, 3 Dutch, 2 Polish, 2 German, 1 Swiss and 1 Swedish.*

with Postmaa, which culminated in the award of his pilot's licence on 14 July, the first such in the Brabant area.

Following a conversion course onto the Coupé, which differed considerably from the Pander EK-80 biplane (nickmamed the 'Goat') which Boon had previously flown, Boon took the aircraft on a trip around the Netherlands on 25-26 August.

A month later Boon was invited to participate in a circuit around France lasting eight days. He was accompanied by 19-year old J.H. von den Nahmer as passenger and navigator. After attending to some minor plywood repairs, the pair started from Welschap on 16 September.

Although plagued by bad weather and occasionally getting lost (Nahmer being a poor navigator according to some) they returned home safely to Eindhoven.

For his part, Bazelmans had also begun flying lessons, again with Postmaa, and by November had also gained his licence on the 'Goat'. Once familiar with the Coupé, he too was keen to stay in the air.

On 30 December 1933 the Fokker F.XVIII, *Pelikaan*, was due back in Holland after a record-breaking flight from the Dutch East Indies (now Indonesia). Bazelmans determined to be at Schiphol to witness this event. As might be expected, the weather was bad, and in the vicinity of Mijdrecht Bazelmans was obliged to make an emergency landing in which he broke a leg, while his passenger, a Mr L. Staals, suffered cuts and bruises. For the aircraft, however, the landing proved fatal and so Coupé PH-BBC met its end. It should be said though, that the rugged plywood construction probably helped save the passengers from more serious injuries, so perhaps the ending was not so inglorious after all.

Extracts from a translation of the official report into the accident, supplied by courtesy of Mr Hermann Dekker, follow:

A SHORT DESCRIPTION OF THE ACCIDENT
The aircraft PH-BBC, piloted by Mr F.C. Bazelmans, took off on 30 December 1933 from the airfield of Eindhoven with the destination of Schiphol. Mr L. Staals was on board as a passenger.

As the pilot was unable to locate the airfield of Schiphol, they decided after some flying about to make an emergency landing on a meadow in the municipality of Mijdrecht.

While attempting to investigate the landing area more closely, the pilot suddenly lost control of his aircraft. The aircraft crashed from a very low altitude onto the meadow and as the aircraft impacted, the pilot was seriously injured, the passenger had no serious injury. The aircraft was, however, seriously damaged.

TYPE OF INVESTIGATION
Following a telephone request from the Aviation

Authority soon after the crash, an inquiry by the local police was undertaken. A few days later a visit was arranged to the place of the accident to verify and conclude the police inquiry and to interrogate witnesses. The wreck of the aircraft had already been removed. The following were questioned;
a   *Mr F.C. Bazelmans*
b   *Mr Th. Meijer*
c   *Mr C. Mulder*
From the last two mentioned persons no deposition was recorded as their statements were identical with those in the police report.

Before the declaration of Mr Bazelmans we refer to the appended supplement 1. The following supplements are also recorded:
2   *A police report into the accident.*
3   *A list of questions to Mr Staals, and his answers thereto.*
4   *A letter from the National Flying School (with enclosure) relating to the aircraft PH-BBC.*
5   *The logbook.*

THE AIRCRAFT
The aircraft is of the Civilian Coupé type, with a Genet Major engine. The English proof of Airworthiness was identical with the similar Dutch Certificate of Airworthiness which was valid until 12 October 1934.

The last inspection by Dutch authorities was on 12 October 1933. The logbook was updated until 9 December 1933. The aircraft had at that date approximately 95 flying hours since it was built.

Enclosure No. 4 shows that the instructor of the National Flying School was of the opinion that this type of aircraft was not suitable for anyone immediately after receiving his licence, although the aircraft itself had no harmful peculiarities.

According to the pilot the aircraft had the habit, when starting or landing to hang over to the right. Also this pilot had the habit when landing of putting the elevator in the raised position.

The first point possibly indicates unfamiliarity with the aircraft; the second that the pilot had acquired the habit of incorrect landing practices.

THE PILOT
The pilot, F.C. Bazelmans, 40 years old, obtained his 'A' Flying Licence on 18 November 1933 but because of incorrect recording in his logbook it could not be ascertained how many hours he had obtained with this aircraft.

From a copy of the letter of 14 December 1933 from the National Flying School to Mr Bazelmans, it appears he had insufficient expwerience to fly this aeroplane.

THE WEATHER CONDITIONS
The weather report for the flying district of Schiphol at the time of the accident was as follows:

28: *The Pander EK-80 biplane, PH-AJB, in which both Boob and Bazelmans learnt to fly. Known as the 'Goat' the aircraft had very different characteristics to the Civilian Coupé which they owned and which caused both some problems on account of their lack of flying experience.*

Hazy visibility 2-4km, sky completely covered with large clouds at a height of 210m, wind on the ground south-westerly 12kmph.

POSSIBLE CAUSES OF THE ACCIDENT

On the morning before the departure Mr Bazelmans performed several landings and starts with the aircraft to reassure himself that both he and the aircraft were in good order, as he had not flown for a month and still had insufficient experience.

Before the departure from Eindhoven, he had obtained the weather report by telephone from Schiphol, which in his opinion seemed in his favour.

The start took place at approximately 1.30 pm. When he arrived in the neighbourhood of Amsterdam, the visibility got gradually worse and as the pilot had lost sight of the ground, he was forced to fly low at about 150-200m.

On account of fog in the Schiphol district, he changed course for Amsterdam, from where he again set course for Schiphol; he was beaten when he could not find the landing ground.

As the search took a long time and as the pilot was afraid of the developing darkness and fuel shortage, he decided to make an emergency landing in a meadow in the parish of Mijdrecht.

Intending to investigate the meadow more closely he flew at a height of 50m and made a left turn. The elevator was already up for the intended landing as was his habit. According to the pilot the engine was running at full power; according to his passenger it was running at low revolutions.

Whatever the situation, the pilot declared that during the turn the engine slowed down and the aircraft began to lose height with its nose downwards. At the same time the aircraft must have turned to the left and turned over as he hit the ground with his left wing, as the tracks on the ground showed.

CONSIDERATIONS OF A POSSIBLE CAUSE

1   The pilot and also his passenger declared that before the accident nothing unusual in the air-

craft or engine was noticed; eyewitnesses declared the same, so it has to be assumed that both aircraft and engine were in airworthy condition.

2   From the statement by the pilot, it appears that the aircraft suddenly lost height. Additionally, from the declaration by the instructor of the National Flying School at Eindhoven (enclosure 4) it may also be assumed that the aircraft at this point had no bad attributes.

3   The raised elevator may have possibly contributed to bringing the aircraft into the described flying attitude. From the information received it is not clear that raising the elevator for landing in this aircraft is necessary.

The pilot had obviously acquired this habit, according to his statement, in order to improve the landing and save on tyre wear.

4   The accident was most likely due to loss of height and speed during the turn. It should be recorded in this connection that, according to the pilot, the margin between cruising and landing speed was minimal.

's-Gravenhage
7 February 1934

Inspector of Aviation Services
(signed) van der Heyden

For the above copy,
The Secretary-General of the Department for Roads and Waterways

THE CIVILIAN COUPÉ MK II
Number 0.2.2. / G-ABFJ & Number 0.2.4.

Despite being listed as the third airframe to be built, this Coupé was actually the second to receive its Certificate of Airworthiness, on 16 April 1931. It was first registered as G-ABFJ to the Civilian Aircraft Company Ltd, Hedon, on 27 September 1930 — which is intriguing as the firm did not officially move there until January 1931. This suggests that the either the company moved to Hedon well before lease negotiations with Hull Corporation were completed (if they ever were), or a 'paper' move was made in anticipation of the actual move or the aircraft was at least partially completed in Burton on Trent.

Along with G-ABFI, -ABFJ competed in the Heston-Cramlington (Newcastle) Race of 30 May 1931. Unfortunately Capt. G.A. Pennington, the pilot, had to make an emergency landing through fuel shortage.

In June, an optimistic RAF pilot, Flt Lt V.S. Bowling, bought the aircraft with a view to flying it in the King's Cup Race to held on the 25 July.

Presumably the sale was not completed or Bowling was unable to fly at the time and allowed Lawrence Dawson, the Civilian Aircraft Company's managing director to fly in his stead, for both aircraft were next entered for the Hanworth-Blackpool Race of 8 July; this time both came down prematurely through engine problems. G-ABFJ ended up on its nose at Sandbach. The damage was serious enough for the aircraft to be struck off the register the same day. As a result Bowling failed to start on 25 July. G-ABFJ was dismantled and never flew again. It was probably used for spares.

G-AFBJ's only other claim to fame is that it was the star of an enthusiastic article and several photographs in the April 10, 1931, issue of *Flight* which extolled its durability and comfort, although it was slightly more reserved about the handling.

Number 0.2.4.

One of the most mysterious of all the Coupés, for unknown reasons this aircraft was never registered. The succeeding machine on the production line went to Germany, but of number 4 — nothing.

The most likely scenario is that the aircraft was built but never completed or assembled and may well have formed part of the large quantity of spares acquired by Joe Gilmore direct from the factory in Hedon after it closed in order to keep Coupé Mk I number 1, EI-AAV, flying.

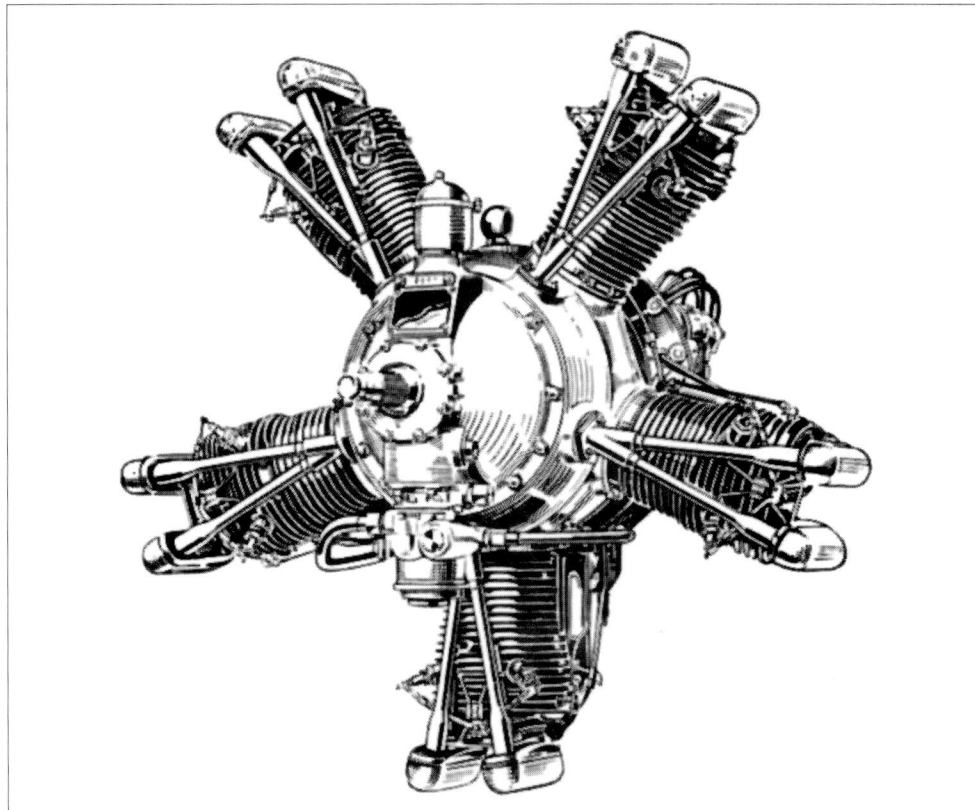

29 : *For a time the Mk I flew with its A.B.C. engine in and extended cowling which gave quite an elegant line to the aircraft (see page 6). In this picture of Mk II G-ABFJ, it can be seen that the designer has moved back to the early rather short-nosed appearance of the first aircraft, even though the engine is now the Genet Major radial.*

30: *A technical drawing of the Armstrong Siddeley five-cylinder Genet Major engine of 110 hp. The extra power over the 75 hp of the Hornet made a great difference to the Coupé's practicality.*

31: *A starboard view of G-ABFJ in flight shows off basically pleasing lines, spoiled only by the rather lumpen vertical tail assembly. An attempt has been made to minimise this effect by painting a sweeping curve to the dark colour of the fin. But how much better might the aircraft have done if it had had a more elegant tail such as that on the De Havilland Puss Moth?*

THE CIVILIAN COUPÉ MK II

Number 0.2.3. / G-ABNT

G-ABNT, works number 0.2.3., was built at Hedon and registered to the Civilian Aircraft Co Ltd., in June 1931. The Certificate of Airworthiness, No. 3199, was issued on 10 September 1931. This notes that the first recorded owner is Henlys Ltd, based at Heston Aerodrome in Middlesex. This may be linked with the hard times which were beginning to afflict the Civilian company.

Nine days later in the Heston-Cardiff race, Flt Lt. Bowling could only manage a tenth place, the aircraft staggering along at 89mph. On 21 May 1932, carying the Number 17, it was entered in the *Morning Post* Air Race at Heston, but it was a non-starter. It was then used as a demonstrator for a while.

By 13 September 1932, the C of A records that it was in the ownership of E.G. Downes Martin of Christchurch, Hants. On 10 February 1933 it passed to S.B. Cliff, then based at Philips & Powis Aircraft at Woodley, near Reading, and later at the former Bristol civil aerodrome, Whitechurch.

S.B. Cliff flew G-ABNT abroad as recorded in the Coupé's *Carnet de Passages en Douanes* to Belgium, to the aerodrome of Saint-Inglevert in France and Aachen (Aix la Chapelle) in Germany.

At about this time a certain Glyn Rhys from Carmarthen in Wales, was keen on flying but as he assisted his father in a grocery store at Waverley, for his keep and what amounted to pocket money, he could not afford to buy a 'plane. He had a flair for window dressing, however, and as a result of display competitions won sufficient money to enable him to start on a course of flying lessons at Cardiff Aero Club, where he asked for a demonstration of the Civilian Coupé.

Dennis Rhys, his surviving younger brother, informed the author that the prototype, G-AAIL, was brought to Pendine beach for a demonsration flight, but Glyn did not like it; the engine leaked oil, the aircraft looked rough and it also took ages to take off. But a later demonstration of the more powerful Mk. II G-ABNT by S.B. Cliff at the Pendine beach, was more to his liking.

Before the year was out, on 26 October 1933, G-ABNT was aquired by Glyn at a cost of £300, who soon nicknamed it 'Bunty'. The aircraft was then based at Cardiff.

Unfortunately, Glyn Rhys was still learning to fly and even when he gained his 'A' licence to fly in biplane Moths (by De Havilland) he was still grounded as far as his own machine was concerned. The accepted wisdom of the time was that the Coupé was considered to be too advanced for a beginner and

33: This is possibly the start of the Heston-Cardiff rce in September 1931 showing G-ABNT in a different and earlier colour scheme of dark blue and silver. It wears a racing number '17' on the tail and a strange marking under the canopy, as the star shape is very similar to the De Havilland Company's emblem but as the aircraft was flown by a serving RAF officer in the race it could also be his squadron badge. The aircraft in the background is an Avro Avian, which wears its company logo under the cockpit.

34: Positive proof that G-ABNT at least was finished in blue and silver as shown by the works order confirming the fact.

CIVILIAN AIRCRAFT CO., LTD.,

AIRPORT OF HULL,

Telegrams: "CIVILIAN, HEDON."
Telephone No.: HEDON, 82.

HEDON, EAST YORKS.

——2nd July,——— 1931

M—— essrs. H. Moses & Sons,

Brook Street,   HULL.

Your Quotation—————— —————

Please supply as under: Carriage————— paid

THIS ORDER NO.

925

MUST BE SHOWN ON
ADVICE NOTE,
INVOICE AND LABEL.

PAINTING IN BLUE AND ALUMINIUM -

ONE CIVILIAN COUPÉ, G-ABNT.

35: G-ABNT looking a little more worn with a different race number on the fin. But which race, and when?

36: 'Bunty' at Splott, Cardiff, date uncertain. Club members were rather in awe of the little Coupé, saying it was too advanced to fly straight from the Gypsy Moth on which Glyn Rhys learnt to fly. Finish now appears to be silver with a white tail.

37: Bunty at Pendine Sands with the Roesch Talbot behind in about 1936 with, from left, Dennis Rhys, his brother Emlyn and Captain Watkiss, the flight engineer at Splott. Wakiss flew Sopwith Pups, Camels and DH 5s in World War I.

37: Filling up with Shell-Mex at the Avola petrol station, Pendine in about 1936. At about 3 shillings a gallon, both car and aircraft benefitted. Behind the carDennis and Emlyn Rhys and Wilfred Morgan, owner of the petrol station. Howard Rhys in 'plus fours' filling up. The Avola building still stands but the pump is no more.

no intermediate type trainer was available.

Rhys, with the impatience of youth, could not wait to gain the freedom of the skies in his own aircraft, so he took a chance one day when his instructor was away from Cardiff aerodrome at Pengam Moors. He taxied up the runway and his Coupé took to the air, much to the alarm of the fire and ambulance men. He recalled later:

"I did however manage to land safely and much to my surprise I was congratulated and ordered to go round again, which I did, but when the instructor returned he was not pleased."

From then on Glyn was allowed to fly the 'plane and on gaining his pilot's licence he flew Bunty at Cardiff. Soon tiring of travelling from Carmarthen to Cardiff, however, he flew on his first cross-country trip from Cardiff to Pendine, where he had planned to keep it. There he arranged to keep the machine in the garage of the Beach Hotel, as the wings could be folded. So for some years Bunty became a permanent resident.

Pendine Sands, the seven-mile long beach, was his airstrip and the aircraft's 20 gallon tank was filled up at the local 'Avola' Garage pump with Shell-Mex petrol. The engine ran surprisingly well on this rather low octane fuel, which cost about three shillings a gallon, in present day money about 15 pence, recalled Dennis Rhys, who had many tales of the adventures he and his brother Glyn had when flying from Pendine.

On one occasion they took Bunty to Hedon to obtain a Certificate of Airworthiness. This was done by Withernsea-based Vincent Lockey, who held an Air Ministry Ground Engineer's licence enabling him to work on several different types of aircraft and engines, including the Coupé. As he also held a pilot's licence he saw both sides of the aircraft, one of only two or three people in the country who had this qualification.

When the Civilian Aircraft Company was bankrupted, Lockey bought all the unfinished and finished parts of the Coupés at the auction. Glyn and Dennis bought spare wings, tailplanes, fuselage and front end etc from him; in fact almost enough to make another aircraft.*

Lockey also supplied Joe Gilmore in Ireland with a wing and a fuselage, as noted in the description of G-AAIL. But back to Bunty:

At one time they were having a race between their Roesch-Talbot convertible car and Bunty when the aircraft flew so low that it dented the car's hood irons.

On another occasion, after meeting heavy weather, they arrived late at Pendine beach to find that the tide was in and as their fuel was low, they were obliged to ditch the machine in the shallows:

"It was a Sunday evening and almost dark, and

The remaining spare parts, namely the unregistered Coupé, works no. 0.2.7., are with the present owner of G-ABNT. Presumably these also included components of 0.2.6, which also remained uncompleted and unregistered.

local folk came out of the chapel in bowler hats and dressed in 'Sunday best' and carried G-ABNT out of the water. They managed to rescue the 'plane, with Glyn and I still in it, by wading into the sea, in some cases up their chests, with no damage to the 'plane. The propeller, however, was damaged, but Bunty did not suffer any ill-effects from the immersion in the sea.

Another fine Sunday we churned Bunty up towards 'Heaven'. (I do not know if Glyn ever prayed but I did very much so always!). Glyn said to me 'I feel groggy', and so did I. That was over my hometown of Carmarthen. We did not realize we needed oxygen but I am told that we recovered!

One foul Sunday morning, Glyn took off from Pendine when the tide was in, the birds were walking and the south-east wind was coming directly from the sea. We pushed Bunty back to the sand dunes and with about four people holding the wing struts on each side, Glyn, with the engine flat-out but with the brakes on signalled to let go but as he was on the left side of the cabin, the folk on the right side did not see the signal. Bunty went off like a scalded cat to the left and over the water, just inches above the waves."

In 1937 Glyn Rhys had to go to London for a student course in Harrod's store. He later returned to Pendine, intending to fly Bunty back to Heston to start the 'Harrods Flying Club'. He made an attempt to fly back to London, but when filling up at Cardiff, the chief engineer at the aerodrome spotted an oil leak and said that the fault should be investigated. Glyn recalled the flight in the aircraft's logbook for 21 February 1937:

"Perfect weather with a tail-wind of about 25 mph at 2,000 feet. Ran motor at 1,800 revs., I found it steady and oil pressure constant at 55."

The aircraft returned to Carmarthen and with the coming of World War II it remained grounded. In the middle of 1939 Glyn sold a complete front structure and engine mounting to Joe Gilmore to restore his aircraft after a crash, but then the war started and Gilmore never paid up. G-ABNT was dismantled and stored in the attic behind the family store in Carmarthen in 1939. Postwar, pressure of business kept Rhys too busy to to restore the aircraft. When the designer inspected it in 1961, he found that the plywood covering and glued joints were as good as ever. Eventually, in 1978, on Glyn Rhys's retirement, the aircraft was sold by auction to a new owner who wished to restore it to flying condition, as will be seen.

Glyn Rhys later recalled of flying in the 'thirties:

"Those were halcyon days with Pendine sands and heavens all to myself, except for, occasionally, Amy Johnson, Jim Mollison and Parry Thomas."

THE CIVILIAN COUPÉ MK II
Number 0.2.5. / G-ABPW / D-EPAN

The fifth, and last, Civilian Coupé Mk II, G-APBW had no actual career in Britain but was ordered and supplied direct from the factory in Hedon to Aachen, Germany. First registered on 16 September 1931, the Certificate of Airworthiness was issued on 27 August the following year. The delivery flight was made via Heston on 14 October 1932, the pilot being S.B. Cliff. The British registration was thereupon cancelled.

According to International Law, the aircraft should then have been re-allocated a German registration. At the time this would have consisted of the letter 'D' followed by four numbers. No record of the precise registration has been found but even if it had, it seems, looking at the accompanying photos, that it might not have been carried in any case.

According to the memoirs of now-retired *Flugkapitän* Richard Perlia, the aircraft was first purchased by a pupil of his, a Mr Winard Gülpen, then owner of a driving school at Düren in the Rhineland. This seems entirely likely as the details of such a driving school can be made out on the fin of the aircraft in the photograph above. It is also apparent from both Perlia's log book and the photos that the British registration was retained while the aircraft was in Germany. Whether this was due to a lack of knowledge of the regulations, a disinclination to do

the necessary repainting or a deliberate subterfuge is not known, but the effect was to apparently convince the German authorities that inspections in accordance with German regulations were not required. This resulted in some interesting escapades as Perlia recounted:

"After successful training, one of my pupils bought himself an aeroplane of his own; a Civilian Coupé, which for that time was a very progressive and elegant aircraft with an enclosed cabin, a braced high-wing monoplane. power source was an air-cooled Genet Major radial engine of 160 hp (sic). Because of its English registration it did not have to comply with the German safety laws and did not have to be inspected regularly, a condition which had dire consequences later.

For us the Coupé was a very good thing. In a high-speed manner we used this aircraft to create 'Flying Days' on any suitable meadow. To attract the visitors we did a little fancy flying; we then started the profitable ten-minute round trips flying our guests over their nearby villages. Furthermore we also used this aircraft for longer journeys for business people who had a pressing engagement and who did not fight shy of flying in a sportsplane.

It so happened that one day a director of the

39: *G-ABPW (or whatever it should have been numbered) in a slightly different finish to the preceding picture with a rather crudely painted registration.*

40: *The German Coupé at te start of a flight from Bonn-Hangelar. This was the home base of the second owner, Ernst Panzer. Presumably it is sometime before May 1934 when it became mandatory to apply the German registration D-EPAN. Judging by the crowd and the uniformed men in the background, the occasion appears to be a DLV sport flying day*

41: *As related in the text, the aircraft was used for an eventful flight intended to end in Barcelona. Here it is during a fuelling stop at Saarbrucken.*

42: *The first forced landing in typical Swiss Jura scenery at La Chaud de Fond. Note the typical leather flying overcoat of the time worn by Perlia.*

"Cologne Ford works had to go quickly to Barcelona in Spain but the fast journey turned into a slow one due to problems.

It began over the Swiss Jura when we had to make the first forced landing. First the engine made some terrible noises and next the prop stood still, and then we were flying in a glider, gliding to earth. I was searching hopefully for a useable landing spot when to my great relief I found that we were over a very small handkerchief-sized airfield at La Chaud where after a short time we were able to land and glad to have terra firma beneath our feet.

The problem was soon found — one piston in a cylinder had seized solid. I dismantled the cylinder, used some emery paper, cleaned and oiled the parts. This procedure was now a routine; we took the required tools on all our journeys and, after a short time, we were airborne again. So far so good; my passenger was pleased with the smooth landing and the quick repair to the engine and looked forward to a fast journey to Barcelona. But soon, over Lake Geneva this time, at a height of only 150 metres, our engine began to stutter again, and then stopped. Suddenly the water was very near indeed. I was very frightened. To put the aircraft down was not the problem — but swimming to the shore? But somehow we reached the shore, touching the shallow water with our wheels to land with our last momentum, fortunately in a suitable dry place.

This time we had landed very close to the Swiss military airport of La Blecherette, and it did not take very long before we were confronted by Swiss soldiers, who wanted to know precisely what we were trying to do in an exclusion zone. It took some time until we succeeded in explaining our predicament, but a quick examination of our engine by our Swiss

hosts soon showed that it had again ceased.

My passenger had had enough. With un-complimentary words he said goodbye, to continue the journey to Barcelona by rail.

Because of the many forced landings we finally decided to sell the Civilian Coupé."

D-EPAN

Following the introduction of new regulations concerning the aircraft registration system, on 27 May 1934, G-ABPW obtained the new-style registration of D-EPAN. This was made up of the initial and the first three letters of the new owner's surname i.e. **E**rnest **Pan**zer, according to the aircraft's logbook which has survived. Another card which accompanies the logbook certifies that D-EPAN is a Member of the D.L.V. (German Airsport Club) and entitled to concessions from the airport authorities. The last entry in the logbook, number 44, states:

"Pilot Eduard Meyerding, (the father-in-law of Mr Panzer) on a local flight, Bonn, on the 6. VII. 35 at 9.16 a.m., crashed at 9:20 at the entrance to the Monastery of St. Augustin, killing the pilot, the 'plane being totally destroyed and written off."

The actual cause of the crash has not yet been established but it would seem that Panzer had not owned the aircraft for long, only a matter of weeks since the middle of June. It is of course possible, given *Flugkapitän* Perlia's comments, that neglect could have caused a mechanical failure of some kind.

The evidence for the eventual fate of D-EPAN would seem pretty conclusive, except for the fact that the aircraft was not struck off the International Aircraft Register until 1939. The most likely explanation was a simple delay in the official paperwork catching up with events, (the German air authorities were going through rapid change and expansion at the time with the accession of the Nazi Party to power) although there still is an outside chance that the aircraft survived and was repaired.

Even so, it has to be noted that this was the only fatality in a crash involving a Civilian aircraft, which perhaps proves that even if blessed with engines which were not the most reliable, the Coupé was an inherently safe and forgiving machine, as those who flew it regularly have stated.

As for Panzer himself, he was born 18 September 1898. He was a Bachelor of Commerce, and had a business in Bonn dealing in car parts, engineering-equipment, metals tools and accessories. He died on 20 August 1990, having reached the ripe old age of 92 years.

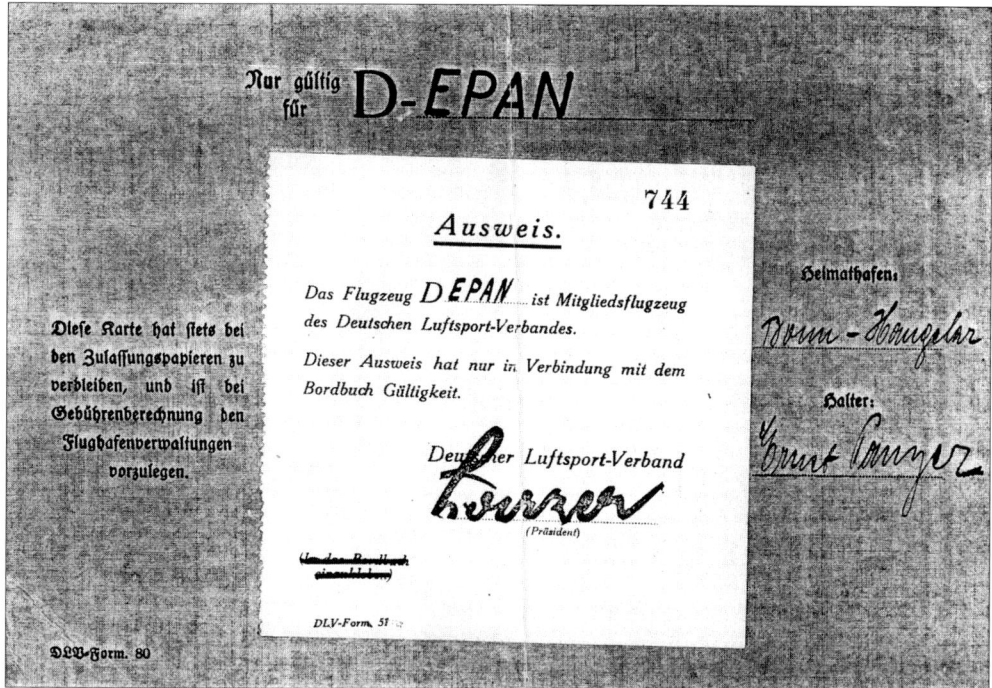

42: The pass confirming the new registration applied to the Coupé in Germany and that the aircraft is now officially part of the civilian Deutscher Luftsports Verband, the predecessor of the NSFK, the political National-sozialistisches Fliegerkorps, which was resurrected in 1937 and absorbed the earlier organisation. The facsimile signature is that of the leader of the DLV, Bruno Loerzer, a First World War fighter ace, and a great friend of Hermann Göring.

43: Ernst Panzer's passport, issued in Bonn.

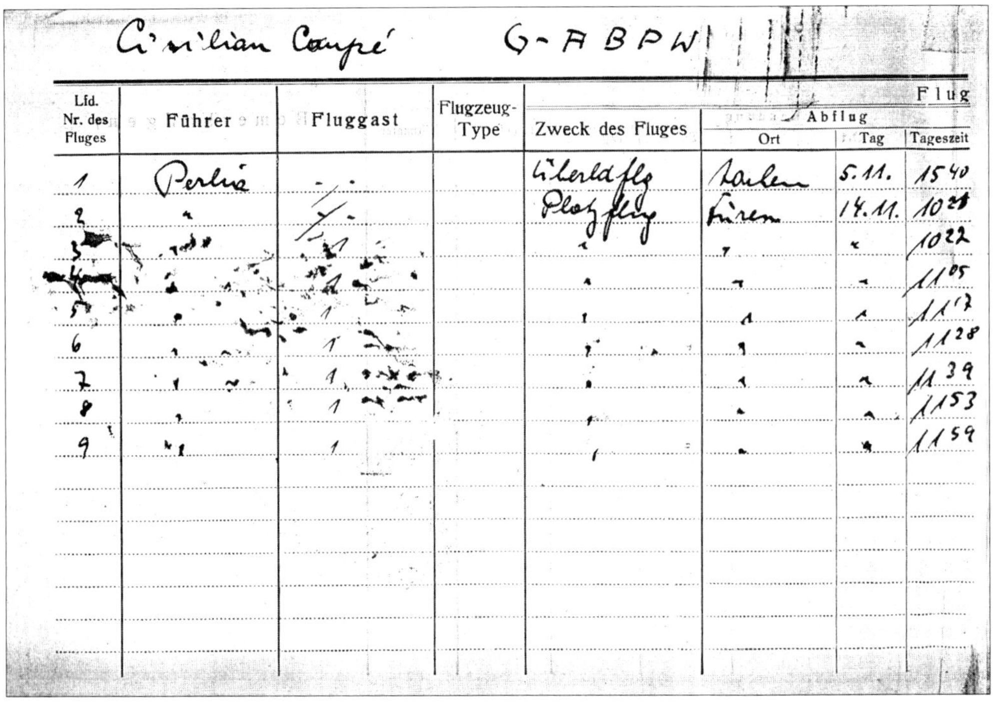

Civilian Coupé G-ABPW

Lfd. Nr. des Fluges	Führer	Fluggast	Flugzeug-Type	Zweck des Fluges	Flug – Abflug: Ort	Tag	Tageszeit
1	Perlia	-/-		Überldflg	Aachen	5.11.	1540
2	"	-/-		Platzflug	Düren	14.11.	1021
3	"	"		"	"	"	1022
4	"	"		"	"	"	1105
5	"	"		"	"	"	1117
6	"	"		"	"	"	1128
7	"	"		"	"	"	1139
8	"	"		"	"	"	1153
9	"	"		"	"	"	1159

44: The left hand pages of Flugkapitän Richard Perlia's log book showing various flights in the Coupé and further confirming that it retained its British registration.

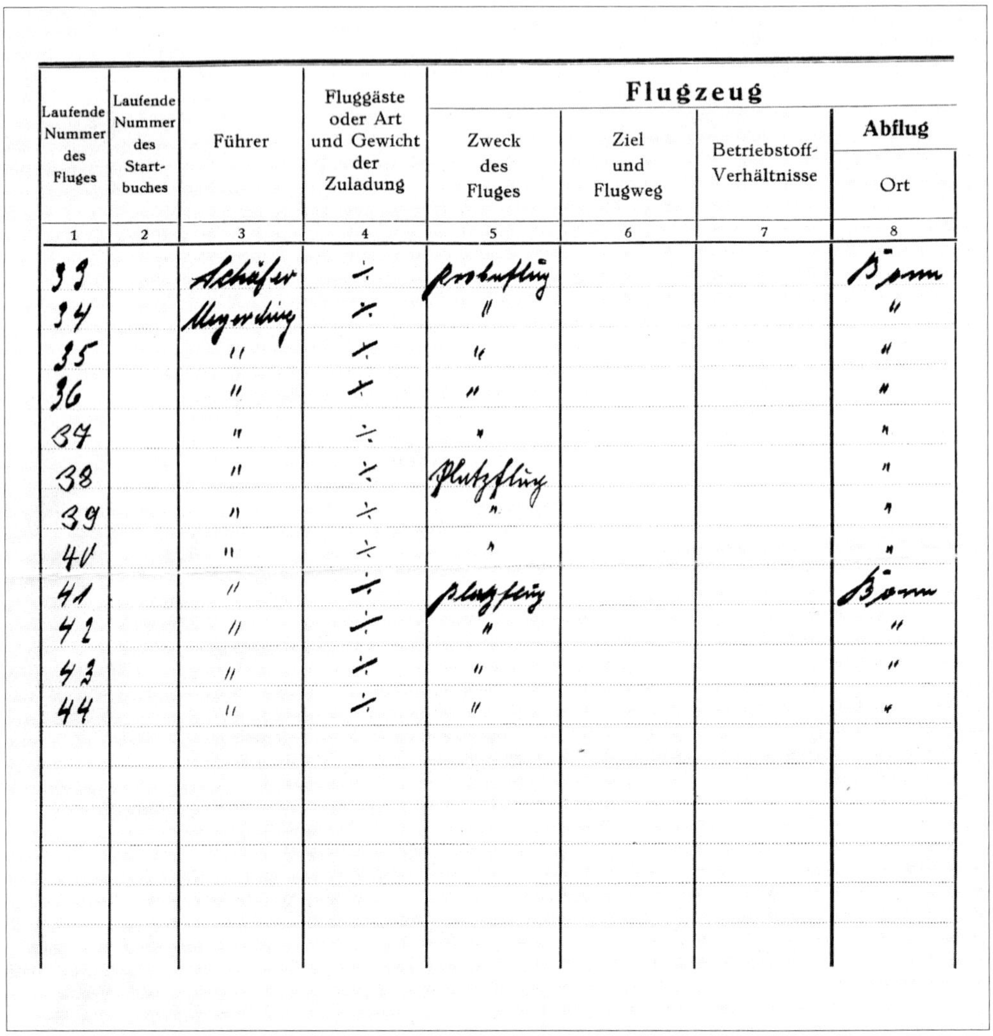

Laufende Nummer des Fluges	Laufende Nummer des Startbuches	Führer	Fluggäste oder Art und Gewicht der Zuladung	Flugzeug: Zweck des Fluges	Ziel und Flugweg	Betriebstoff-Verhältnisse	Abflug: Ort
1	2	3	4	5	6	7	8
33		Schäfer	-/-	Probeflug			Bonn
34		Meyerding	-/-	"			"
35		"	-/-	"			"
36		"	-/-	"			"
37		"	-/-	"			"
38		"	-/-	Platzflug			"
39		"	-/-	"			"
40		"	-/-	"			"
41		"	-/-	Platzflug			Bonn
42		"	-/-	"			"
43		"	-/-	"			"
44		"	-/-	"			"

45: The similar page from the log book of D-EPAN showing flights 33-44, the last one. The first flight as D-EPAN took place on 27 May 1934 and there were only 32 flights prior to those noted here which begin on 16 June 1935. All are from its home base at Bonn-Hangelar. Most were flown by Eduard Meyerding, Ernst Panzer's father-in-law.

46: *The right hand page of Richard Perlia's log book confirming that the first flights by 0.2.5 in Germany were from Düren.*

47: *The right hand page of D-EPAN's log book showing that it was not flown extensively in the month before the fatal crash in which Meyerding was killed and the aircraft written off. The last handwritten note records the place and time of the crash: the monastery of St. Augustin at 09.20 hours.*

A	B	C		D	MUSTER	E	F	MUSTER	G
Nr. A.I.R.	EINTRAGUNGSZEICHEN	KLASSIFIKATION		FLUGZEUG		AENDERUNGEN	MOTOREN		BRENNSTOFFVORRAT IN L.
	NAME	FLUGGÄSTE	BESATZUNG	ERBAUER			ERBAUER		ELEKTRISCHE AUSRÜSTUNG
Nr.D. ZULASSUNGS-BESCHEINIGUNG	EIGENTÜMER			WERKNUMMER		GEGENÜBER	ZÜNDUNG	KÜHLUNG	INSTRUMENTE HEIZUNG
	WOHNORT	RÜSTGEW.	FLUGGEWICHT	DAUORT			ANLASSER	LUFTSCHRAUBE	FEUERSCHUTZEINRICHTUNGEN
AUSSTELL. DATUM	HEIMATSHAFEN	FLUGWEITE IN KM.		DAUJAHR		DEM MUSTERFLUGZEUG			NOTAUSGAENGE
1-80235	D-EORY	....	N Se	Bü	133 C	....	Sh	14 A	105
	.... [für Luftfahrt e. V.			Bücker Flugzeugbau			Brandenburgische	[Motorenwerke	....
D-EORY	Deutsche Versuchsanstalt	1	1				Mg	A	Cl. prf.
	Berlin-Adlershof	420	630	Rangsdorf			Mgd		
....	Adlershof	....							
1-80335	D-EOVU	....	N ES	He	72 D	....	Sh	14 a	150
	.... [für Luftfahrt e. V.			Ernst Heinkel Flugzeugwerke			Brandenburgische	[Motorenwerke	....
D-EOVU	Deutsche Versuchsanstalt	1	1				Mg	A	Cl. prf.
	Berlin-Adlershof	525	900	Rostock			Mgd		
....	Adlershof	....							
1-80377	D-EOXK	....	N Se	Bü	133 C	....	Sh	14 A	105
	....			Bücker Flugzeugbau			Brandenburgische	[Motorenwerke	....
D-EOXK	NS.-Fliegerkorps	1	1				Mg	A	Cl. prf.
	Berlin	420	630	Rangsdorf			Mgd		
....	....	....							
1-80433	D-EOZO	....	N ES	FW	44 J	....	Sh	14	135
	.... [für Luftfahrt e.V.			Focke-Wulf Flugzeugbau			Brandenburgische	[Motorenwerke	....
D-EOZO	Deutsche Versuchsanstalt	1	1				Mg	A	Cl. prf.
	Berlin-Adlershof	565	900	Bremen			Mgd		
....	Adlershof	....							
1-80450	D-EPAF	....	N Se	L	25 d VII R	....	HM	60 R	90
	....			Leichtflugzeugbau Klemm			Hirth Motor. n Ges.		....
D-EPAF	NS.-Fliegerkorps	1	1				Mg	A	Cl. prf.
	Mannheim	390	720	Böblingen			Mgd		
....	Neuostheim	....							
1-80455	D-EPAK	....	N Se	L	25 c VII	....	HM	60	90
	....			Leichtflugzeugbau Klemm			Hirth Motoren Ges.		....
D-EPAK	NS.-Fliegerkorps	1	1				Mg	A	Cl. prf.
	Berlin W 35	420	650	Böblingen			Mgd		
... .	....	....							
1-80458	D-EPAN	....	....	Civilian	Coupe Ser. O 2	....	Genet	Major	....
	....			....			....		....
D-EPAN	Ernst Panzer	....	....	....			....		
	Bonn/a. Rh.	....		....			....		
....	Hangelar								
1-80459	D-EPAO	....	N Se	Kl	35 A	....	HM	60 R	90
	....			Leichtflugzeugbau Klemm			Hirth Motoren Ges.		....
D-EPAO	NS.-Fliegerkorps	2	1				Mg	A	Cl. prf.
	Berlin	380	705	Böblingen			Mgd		
....	....	....							
1-80460	D-EPAP	....	N Se	He	72 D	....	Sh	14 A	150
	....			Ernst Heinkel Flugzeugwerke			Brandenburgische	[Motorenwerke	....
D-EPAP	NS.-Fliegerkorps	1	1				Mg	A	Cl. prf.
	Berlin W 35	525	900	Rostock			Mgd		
....	....								

ASSOCIATION INTERNATIONALE

A·I·R

DES REGISTRES

THE CIVILIAN COUPÉ MK II
Numbers O.2.6. & O.2.7.

Probably on account of the parlous state of the Civilian Aircraft Company these two aircraft were never registered, and never completed. Both probably formed part of the large quantity of spares acquired by Glyn Rhys from Vincent Lockey after the factory closed in order to keep his own aircraft, G-ABNT, flying. Certainly parts of O.2.7. are still held by Shipping and Airlines Ltd.

48: The official record for D-EPAN showing the name and location of the aircraft. It is noteworthy that every aircraft apart from D-EPAN is owned by one Government organisation or another. Ultimately D-EPAN was taken over by the DLV which in turn was eventually taken over by the Nazi Party. The second letter, 'E', in the registration of every aircraft listed shows them to be landplanes of Class A2, with an all-up weight of no more than 1,000 kg and capable of carrying 1-3 people.

49: The emblem of the International Air Registration Association, with which G-ABPW should have logged its first German registration, consisting of the letter 'D' and four numbers, which it apparently never wore. The A.I.R. did, however, hold a record of the second such registration.

THE SURVIVOR
G-ABNT, the last of the Mohicans

50: *Reborn and resplendent in a silver and blue colour scheme, G-ABNT on display in front of a large crowd at Duxford where this unique aircraft was auctioned by Christies on 28 April 1990, when it realised £32,000. The new owner was Michael Dunkerley who still owns the aircraft. At the time of purchase, fitted with 100 hp Genet Major 1A engine number 9151, the aircraft had flown 135 hours. By May 2003 her total flight time was 175 hours 05 minutes.*

G-ABNT, works number 0.2.3., was taken to pieces and stored in the attic by its then owner, Glyn Rhys, in 1939. Almost forty years later, in 1978, still in the attic, the aircraft was auctioned off as it stood by the local auctioneers, John Francis, Thomas Jones and Sons, on the occasion of Glyn Rhys's retirement.

One of many items sold when the family store was auctioned off on Thursday, 9 February, the aircraft was expected to fetch an estimated price in excess of £2,000.

When asked for his feelings about the aircraft Rhys commented:

"I was head over heels in love with it — I still am — I believe it is an interesting example of the enterprise of that era. Had the Hull company not faded away, I think the Coupé could have become the man in the street's aeroplane. It was lovely to fly, with no vices. I have many happy memories and I am very sorry to see it go."

The successful bidder, who paid £3,500 for it was millionaire Phillip Mann. 'Bunty' was despatched to Biggin Hill for restoration, where it took eleven months and £50,000 for it to be brought back to flying condition.

Rather later Michael Dunkerley bought Mann's company, Shipping and Airlines Ltd, the assets of which included G-ABNT. The Coupé thus joined Dunkerley's collection of other vintage aircraft.

At the time of purchase of the Coupé his favourite aircraft was actually a bright yellow Grumman Widgeon amphibian. Commenting upon his latest acquisition:

"It would be nice if the Coupé was in some sort of collection, flying regularly for people to see, but it would require some form of sponsorship. It seems rather selfish for a private person to have it. It really ought to be in Hull or Wales with an agreement that it flew once or twice a month."

He also owns the remains of another Coupé, works number 0.2.7, an unfinished example which was never registered. Somewhere among all the spare parts which he bought could also be components of the 'missing' 0.2.6. Or did they go to Ireland?

In June 1987, more than fifty years after they first acquired their beloved aircraft, Glyn and Dennis Rhys travelled to Biggin Hill, by bus, to view the newly reborn machine.

After restoration by Tony Habgood, the magnificently restored little machine was awarded the Concours d'Elegance at the Brooklands Air Festival on 3 September 1995. At the time of writing G-ABNT remains the only aircraft of its type left in the world but still flies regularly for people to see and admire as an example of what was once the leading edge of aircraft design.

51: 'Bunty' in 1978, dismantled and stored in the attic of the family store in Carmarthen, shortly before it was auctioned off to Phillip Mann. The rugged plywood construction served to keep the aircraft in restorable condition for more than forty years. A pensive looking Glyn Rhys, also forty years older, holds the two-bladed wooden propeller.

52: An unusual recent aerial view of G-ABNT in flight near its home base of Biggin Hill aerodrome in Kent.

53: The paint scheme worn by Bunty these days is based upon that worn by earlier aircraft in the production run, although G-ABNT herself originally had an all-dark blue fuselage, as seen on page 33.

54: *Bunty in her element against a dramatic sky background where few people get to see how the aircraft handles. Note the vintage spoked wheels which were actually worn by all the other Coupés, but which were hidden with lightweight covers.*

55: *The diminutive Coupé compared for size with a restored Hawker Hind which was still in front line service with the RAF in 1936. The monoplane was still a bit new for the air force of the time...*

56: *An overhead view of Bunty glittering in the sunlight and showing off the overhead transparent windows to the cabin. The wing planform has a remarkable resemblance to that of the much later Cessna O-1 Bird Dog.*

GREAT BRITAIN.

———

AIR MINISTRY.

———

CERTIFICATE OF AIRWORTHINESS No. 3199
(Heavier than air.)

FIRST PART.

FULL NAME, ADDRESS AND NATIONALITY OF OWNER OR OF OWNING COMPANY.

1. Surname of owner (or name of Company) : ~~Kemp's Ltd.~~ ~~Downes-Martin~~ ~~Cliff~~ REES
2. Christian name : ~~Stephen Bertram~~ ~~Edward Gawin.~~ Glyn Owen
3. Address : ~~c/o Phillips & Powis Aircraft (Reading) Ltd., Reading Aerodrome,~~ ~~Heston Aerodrome, Hounslow, Middlesex.~~ Woodley, Berks. ~~Avon Wharf, Christchurch, Hants.~~
4. Nationality : British. The Waverley, Lammas Street, Carmarthen, S. Wales.

NAME OF CONSTRUCTOR.

5. Name : Civilian Aircraft Co. Ltd.

NATIONALITY AND REGISTRATION MARKS.

6. .... G-ABNT

DESCRIPTION OF AIRCRAFT.

7. Type Civilian Coupe   Series O.2   Constructor's No. 3
8. Place and year of construction of aircraft : Hedon, East Yorks, 1931.

Class of Aircraft.

9. Land and/or marine : Land.
10. Number of planes : One.
11. Number of engines : One.
12. Maximum number of persons to be carried (including crew) : Two.

Classification of Aircraft.

13. Category : *Normal
14. Subdivision : (d) Private.

*For definition of Normal category see Air Navigation Directions ~~1930 (A.N.D.10)~~ paragraph ~~36~~ (Note 1.)
1932 (A.N.D.11)   37

15. Maximum span (in flying position) : 35' 6"
16. Maximum length (in flying position) : 20' 2"
17. Total height (with and without trolley in case of seaplanes) : 6' 6"

(*1998—544) Wt. 12187—880 750 (2 kds.) 9/30 T.S. 118
(*2003—544) Wt. 14227—1013 7,500 (2 kds.) 10/30 T.S. 118

57: *This purchase order of 2 July 1931 from the Civilian Aircraft Company to Messrs H. Moses and Sons of Brook Street, Hull, covers the upholstering to G-ABNT. As the same company was also commissioned to paint the aircraft, they were presumably a specialist firm of coachbuilders and finishers. The order is signed by Harold Boultbee.*

CIVILIAN AIRCRAFT CO., LTD.,

AIRPORT OF HULL,

Telegrams : " CIVILIAN, HEDON."
Telephone No. : HEDON, 82.

HEDON, EAST YORKS.

THIS ORDER NO.

926

MUST BE SHOWN ON ADVICE NOTE, INVOICE AND LABEL.

2nd July, 193 1

M essrs. H. Moses & Sons,

Brook Street, HULL.

Your Quotation

Please supply as under :

Carriage paid

UPHOLSTERING ONE CIVILIAN COUPÉ, G-ABNT.

All goods to be consigned to Hull Central Station per L.N.E.R. Route.

p.p. THE CIVILIAN AIRCRAFT CO., LTD.

Director.

P.T.O.

58: *A frontal view of G-ABNT outside one of the hangars at Biggin Hill where it now lives.*

"You, the pilot of experience, and you, the complete novice, will, I believe, alike find in the Civilian Coupe an aircraft suited to your needs.

Experience as a designer has taught me how fatally easy it is to sacrifice one good quality to another—controllability to performance, comfort to view, ruggedness of structure to low weight. In the design of the Civilian Coupe I determined that there would be no single point which the critic could select as having been neglected. You, the user, cannot know of the long process of elimination and repeated compromise which is necessary before so ambitious an aim is achieved.

But you can, and, I hope, will, by study of the specification, and by actual flight trials, satisfy yourself that the Civilian Coupe has fulfilled the object that inspired its design,—and justified our claim that it is the most practical light aircraft in existence to-day."

Harold. D. Boultbee

G-ABFJ

ACKNOWLEDGMENTS

About the author

The author would like to express his appreciation of the help provided by the following people, without which the many small pieces which make up the Civilian jigsaw puzzle would not have fallen into place. In England; Dennis Rhys, N.A. Lockey, Charles Boyce, John Mellor, R.J. Bourne, Tony Habgood and Ted Richardson. In Ireland; Paul Cunniffe and George Flood. In the Netherlands; Herman Dekker, Ary Ceelen, Theo Wesselink and Thijs Postma. In Germany; The Deutsches Museum, Hartmut Küper and Richard Perlia. Many others gave encouragement. My heartfelt thanks to you all.

The author

Eduard Friedrich Winkler was born in Hamburg on 4 December 1920. He has had a lifelong enthusiasm for aviation, fostered by an apprenticeship with the German aircraft and shipping firm Blohm and Voss and much hard work in the DLV, followed by call-up into the Luftwaffe in 1942 as an armourer. After recall to Germany in summer 1944 to help install cannons into Messerschmitt Me 262 jets, he was returned to duty as a paratrooper, in which role he was captured at Winnekendonk on the banks of the Rhine on 2 March 1945. Brought to England as a prisoner in 1946, he was finally released on New Year's Eve, 1948. He has remained and worked in England ever since, still enjoying his interest in researching and writing about aviation. He does not wear plus-fours.

59 Above: Harold Boultbee in full period dress extolling the virtues of his aeroplane in a brochure dating from about late 1930.

60: Flieger Winkler in Luftwaffe dress with dark green collar patches with white piping indicating his membership of the Luftwaffe ground troops.